CHEMICAL AND BIOLOGICAL WARFARE

REVISED EDITION

REVISED EDITION

CHEMICAL

AND

BIOLOGICAL WARFARE

C.L. TAYLOR AND L.B. TAYLOR, JR.

Franklin Watts
New York Chicago London Toronto Sydney
An Impact Book

Photographs copyright ©: AP/Wide World Photos: pp. 1, 6, 8, 9, 10, 12, 16; Veterans of Foreign Wars: pp. 2, 11; U.S. Army Photo: pp. 3, 4, 5; Library of Congress: p. 7; Gamma-Liaison: pp. 13 (Tommy Oesterlund), 14 (Jean); UPI/Bettmann Newsphotos: p. 15.

Library of Congress Cataloging-in-Publication Data

Taylor, L. B.
Chemical and biological warfare / L.B. Taylor, Jr. and C. L. Taylor. — Rev. ed.
Includes bibliographical references (p.   ) and index.
Summary: Describes the development and use of chemical and biological weapons throughout history, particularly in the twentieth century.
ISBN 0-531-13029-0
1. Chemical warfare—Juvenile literature.   2. Biological warfare—Juvenile literature.   [1. Chemical warfare.   2. Biological warfare.]   I. Taylor, C. L.   II. Title.
UG447.T39   1992
358′.34—dc20   92-17083
                                                                   CIP   AC

CONTENTS

A PRECEDENT-SETTING ACCORD

On June 1, 1990, President George Bush of the United States and President Mikhail Gorbachev of the Soviet Union met in the East Room of the White House to sign a historic agreement in the quest for international arms control. After a twenty-year struggle over the development and use of chemical weapons arsenals by the superpowers, the two leaders formalized an accord that called for a near-total ban on such weapons. The terms included a complete halt in the production of chemical agents and munitions by the two nations, destruction of the bulk of current stockpiles, and on-site verification of treaty compliance. The pact appeared to bring to a close a troublesome era of U.S.–Soviet tension over chemical arms and was hailed by many experts as a critical step toward a multilateral, global treaty eliminating chemical warfare.

Less than three months later, thousands of allied soldiers donned gas masks and heavy protective gear in the sweltering Saudi desert to prepare themselves against a potential Iraqi offensive using chemical and biological weapons. Following intervention by the U.S.-led coalition forces in the aftermath of Iraq's invasion of Kuwait in August 1990, allied units were required to undergo brutal desert training wearing the cumbersome gear, including heavy suits, gloves, rubber hoods, and respirators. Many succumbed within hours to heat stress during the exercises.

U.S. and British soldiers stationed in the Persian Gulf also received vaccinations against anthrax, a biological weapons threat that Western intelligence agencies had indicated Iraq was capable of introducing during the conflict.[1] In January 1991, U.S. citizens watched live television accounts of Iraqi Scud missile attacks on Israel and Saudi Arabia. Their main fear was that the Scuds might carry chemical warheads.

Despite President Saddam Hussein's repeated threats regarding his military's capacity and willingness to use chemical and biological warfare (CBW), Iraq ultimately refrained from launching such an initiative. Still, Iraq had an incriminating history of using nerve and mustard gas during the 1980s—against Iran during an eight-year war, and later, in several horrifying episodes, against its own Kurdish population in northern Iraq. Thousands of women and children were among the victims.

BREACHING THE MORAL BARRIER

Iraqi use of chemical and biological warfare over the last decade and its threat to launch such an attack during the Persian Gulf War are chilling reminders that the resolution of the 1990 pact between the United States and the Soviet Union was only a single step toward a global accord eliminating this gruesome form of warfare. The documented rise in CBW capabilities in general by Third World nations is a continued threat to world peace. "The Gulf War has once again raised the specter of chemical weapons," President Bush said in May 1991, "and demonstrated that unscrupulous regimes can and will threaten innocent populations with these weapons of terror so long as we permit them to exist. These stark events renew and reinforce my conviction . . . that chemical weapons must be banned everywhere in the world."

Under the terms of United Nations resolutions following the Persian Gulf War, Iraq agreed to destroy its CBW arsenals. Its stockpile has been estimated to include over 46,000 chemical shells and warheads. (Iraq originally reported 10,000 to 11,000 to the U.N. commission overseeing elimination of its weapons arsenal, but this estimate was soon increased by the U.N. inspection teams.)[2] Iraq's chemical stock includes several hundred tons of mustard gas and the nerve agents sarin and tabun. It is interesting to note that sarin and tabun were developed by Germany during World War II but never used.

Iran, Syria, Libya, Egypt, Israel, China, and potentially as many as two dozen other nations possess chemical and biological warfare capabilities, including extensive stockpiles, delivery systems, and production facilities—often created with the aid of Western nations willing to export advanced technological expertise. Finding chemical and biological weapons far less expensive and easier to produce and disguise, these countries have turned to CBW as a credible substitute for nuclear arms—capable of mass destruction and effective in instilling fear and hesitation in potential enemy forces.

"Chemical weapons are thought to offer a cheap and readily obtainable means of redressing the military balance against more powerful foes," stated CIA director William Webster while testifying before the U.S. Senate Foreign Relations Committee in March 1989. "Some see them as the poor man's answer to nuclear weapons. Many countries are developing mustard gas, a terrible weapon first used in World War I. It is a favorite chemical agent for several reasons: its relative ease of manufacture; its long life in storage and on the battlefield; and its ability to incapacitate those who are exposed to it.

"Some countries are also developing nerve agents," Webster added. "These agents, though more difficult to manufacture, can cause death by attacking the brain and nervous system. Other nations may use common industrial chemicals, such as cyanide and phosgene. Cyanide prevents the blood from carrying oxygen, while phosgene, widely used in making plastics, can destroy the lungs."

Webster also registered the agency's concern over the proliferation of biological weapons, even though the Biological Weapons Convention of 1972, which has been signed by 110 nations, bans their production, storage, and use on a global basis. "We are concerned that the moral barrier to biological warfare has been breached," he stated. "At least ten countries are working to produce both previously known and futuristic biological weapons. Biological warfare agents—including toxins—are more potent than the most deadly chemical warfare agents, and provide the broadest area coverage per pound of payload of any weapon system.

"The equipment used to produce biological warfare agents is truly dual use in nature," he continued. "With currently available technology, biological warfare agents can be produced at such a rate that stockpiles are no longer as essential as in the past. . . . Any nation with a modestly developed pharmaceutical industry can produce biological warfare agents, if it chooses."[3]

THE DETERRENCE FACTOR

Not only are Third World nations rapidly establishing chemical and biological arsenals, they have been reluctant to consent to a multilateral accord that would require complete destruction of current stockpiles and the ability to manufacture and store these weapons. Unless nuclear capabilities are also banned, leaders of Third World nations argue, they have a legitimate claim to possess chemical and biological weapons. Foreign Minister Tariq Aziz of Iraq, for example, told representatives of 149 nations attending the Paris Conference on the Prohibition of Chemical Weapons in January 1989 that "Iraq feels that any appeal for total prohibition of chemical weapons should be joined to an identical appeal for total prohibition of nuclear weapons."[4] Syria voiced a similar concern.

The lack of willingness on the part of many smaller nations to abandon their chemical arsenals is among the chief obstacles confronting the United States and the former republics of the Soviet Union as they carry out the terms of the bilateral treaty and work toward its final objective: total elimination of the chemical arsenals held by the two nations. The accord included a provision that enabled the two to retain up to 500 tons of nerve gas (approximately 2 percent of the current U.S. stockpile), until all nations capable of producing chemical weapons ratify a global agreement. This potentially means every nation in the world.

Still, Elisa D. Harris, senior research analyst at the Brookings Institution in Washington, D.C., points out: "The principal value of the bilateral agreement resides in its influence on the prospects for completing and implementing the multilateral treaty. These efforts will be given a powerful political boost by the willingness of the superpowers to forgo any production of chemical weapons in the future and to destroy the vast majority of their chemical arsenals."[5]

The issue of verification is viewed by many analysts as the most serious threat to the U.S.–Soviet accord, and remains the primary obstacle in the multilateral chemical weapons disarmament talks as well. "There is no way to determine that the Soviet declaration concerning the size of the U.S.S.R.'s chemical stockpile is accurate," writes Frank J. Gaffney, Jr., director of the Center for Security Policy and a former Pentagon official. Without a clear indication of the size of the current Soviet arsenal, there is no verifiable means of determining the remaining stockpile once destruction has begun taking place. "Given the ease with which chemical agents can be produced covertly," Gaffney adds, "the likelihood is that only law-abiding nations like the United States will actually be constrained by its limitations."[6]

Harris counters by noting that "the bilateral agreement should not be judged on the basis of verification alone. . . . The Soviet Union is undertaking a legally binding commitment to destroy between 35,000 and 45,000 tons of chemical warfare agent that it otherwise would have retained. . . . This represents a majority of the Soviet chemical stockpile.

"The United States," she adds, "by comparison is undertaking very little in the way of new obligations. The Pentagon is already required under existing law to destroy more chemical weapons by 1997 than it will under the bilateral agreement. Moreover, Congress was unlikely to continue funding the so-called binary weapons program, even in the absence of the U.S.–Soviet deal. . . . Chemical weapons are not needed to deter developing countries that possess these weapons. The United States has overwhelming conventional superiority that can be brought to bear against such countries."[7]

A BILATERAL BREAKTHROUGH

Though chemical arms experts disagree over the value and practicality of the U.S.–Soviet pact, the agreement clearly represents a sharp reversal in the superpowers' positions in the volatile era of previous decades. This was an era of dramatically escalating tensions during a period of suspected Soviet use of chemical weapons and toxins in Southeast Asia and Afghanistan in an effort to quell rebel forces. Estimates of civilian and rebel casualties due to the alleged Soviet CBW offensives from 1975 through 1984 have been greatly debated, but in early 1982, Secretary of State Alexander Haig announced that information obtained by the U.S. government indicated that over 10,000 had been killed and thousands more injured.

Though U.S. administrations found Soviet use of chemical arms during this period difficult to document and quantify (later admitting that much of the evidence was, in fact, inconclusive), the reports and testimony of victims and witnesses enraged senior officials. Use of poison gas was a direct violation of the 1925 Geneva Protocol, prohibiting the use of chemical weapons, which has been signed by the United States and the Soviet Union along with 127 other nations.

In response to the suspected Soviet-backed atrocities in Southeast Asia, President Ronald Reagan began to support Pentagon recommendations to update the nation's chemical arms stock. In 1987, after receiving congressional approval two years earlier, the United States began production of binary nerve gas arms—among the deadliest of chemical weapons. This renewal of chemical weapons production followed a suspension—originally ordered by President Richard Nixon in 1969 and upheld by the Ford and Carter administrations—that had endured for eighteen years.

U.S. production of binary nerve gas weapons continued until the U.S.–Soviet agreement was signed in 1990. By that time, the U.S. arsenal was estimated to include over 25,000 tons of chemical agents, although the Department of Defense had been mandated by Congress to destroy at least 90 percent of the existing stockpile of unitary chemical weapons by 1997. The Soviets claimed to have stockpiles equaling approximately 50,000 tons of agents.

SAFEGUARDING THE ENVIRONMENT

With mandates from Congress and the bilateral agreement calling for large-scale destruction of chemical agents and munitions throughout the next decade, the U.S. Army, charged with chemical weapons elimination, must also concern itself with achieving environmentally sound methods of disposal.

Army plans for destruction of chemical weapons arsenals call for incineration at Johnston Atoll in the South Pacific and at eight sites in the continental United States. Environmentalists, including the organization Greenpeace, have warned, however, that both transport and incineration of these weapons could have long-term, damaging consequences for the environment.

The Soviet Union was faced with similar opposition to its own efforts at chemical weapons elimination, with its destruction facility at Chapayevsk closed due to the protests of local citizens. Both nations agreed to share information on "safe and environmentally sound" methods of destruction as a part of the 1990 pact, yet the process of ridding the arsenals of chemical weapons appears to be as formidable a task as arriving at the agreement itself.

"Although a ban on chemical weapons will not halt the terrible destructiveness of modern warfare," writes John Isaacs, legislative director of the Council for a Livable World, a Washington, D.C.–based lobbying group, "it is essential to draw a line on the battlefield between conventional weapons and weapons of mass destruction—chemical, biological, and nuclear. Eliminating chemical weapons is important because they kill indiscriminately, without warning, and in a most cruel fashion."[8]

Since their modern introduction by Germany during World War I, chemical weapons have earned a legacy worthy of Isaacs's description—providing an insidious, gruesome means of attack that often kills or maims innocent civilians and debilitates whole villages and towns. Today, although the superpowers have cooperated in a landmark chemical arms control agreement and thirty-nine nations are actively participating in the Geneva-based negotiations aimed at a global ban, CBW continues to be among the most disturbing military buildup trends.

Speaking in Aspen, Colorado, in August 1990, President Bush admitted, "In spite of our best efforts to control the spread of chemical and nuclear weapons and ballistic missile technologies, more nations—more, not less, are acquiring weapons of mass destruction and the means to deliver them." Underscoring Bush Administration concern following the Persian Gulf War, the U.S. Army Corps of Engineers announced plans to construct a $20 million chemical weapons research facility at Aberdeen Proving Ground in Harford County, Maryland. The center will advance U.S. efforts in developing protective measures against chemical weapons and determining their effect.[9]

The many barriers to a total banishment of these weapons include the dramatic rise in Third World nation CBW capabilities—due in part to the increased availability of technology and ingredients in spite of restrictive export agreements, and the ease with which these weapons can be manufactured. An alarming potential for terrorist use also exists; environmental concerns continue to constrain arms elimination efforts, and negotiating nations have yet to agree upon effective verification procedures.

The critical question remains: Will the Geneva negotiations succeed in reversing this frightening trend through strict global agreement, or will the horrors of chemical and biological weapons attacks become a frequent reality—not even limited to war?

1. "Fears of Bio-Warfare," *Newsweek*, 27 August 1990, 4.

2. Frank J. Prial, "Iraq Disclosed Only One-Quarter of Its Chemical Arms, U.N. Finds," *The New York Times*, July 31, 1991, 1.

3. Senate Committee on Foreign Relations, "Chemical and Biological Weapons Threats: The Urgent Need for Remedies," January 24, March 1, and May 9, 1989, S. Hrg. 101–252, 29–30.

4. *Washington Post*, 13 January 1989.

5. "Obstacles to Bio-Chemical Disarmament," *Editorial Research Reports*, 29 June 1990, 377.

6. Ibid.

7. Ibid.

8. John Isaacs, "Banning Chemical Weapons," *Technology Review* (October 1990): 34.

9. Kevin L. McQuaid, "New Chemical Weapon Site To Go To Aberdeen," *Baltimore Business Journal*, 25–31 October, 1991, 6.

THE HORROR
AT YPRES

At five o'clock on the afternoon of April 22, 1915, shelling at Langemarck near the Belgian village of Ypres had stopped. The front was quiet. The World War I Allied soldiers were tired after the daylong artillery bout with the Germans, and they lay heavily in their trenches during the respite.

Suddenly the Germans began another deafening round of shelling from their position in the south. Seconds later, the Allied soldiers noticed two greenish-yellow clouds a few hundred yards in front of them. Hanging low on the horizon, the clouds were rapidly approaching them from the German line, and within one minute they had reached the first Allied troops. The men quickly fell into a state of confusion; they were completely unprepared and unprotected for what was to be a devastating poison gas attack.

The gas instantly caused severe burning in their throats and lungs. The men clutched at their chests, coughed, and gasped for breath. Attempts to shield themselves from the gas were largely futile. Many tried to burrow their noses and mouths, or to cover them with cloth, but the moist, dense poison penetrated everything. Others tried to outrun the clouds, inevitably receiving lethal doses as running made them inhale even more deeply. Most fell, choking, their panic turning to agony.

The gas causing these profound, immediate effects was chlorine. The Germans, having waited for the appropriate change in wind direction, had released 160 tons of liquid chlorine from nearly 6,000 pressurized cylinders. On release the chlorine formed a thick, odorous gas cloud. Because of its form, it was impossible to control the direction of the weapon. The Germans had waited for days to release the chlorine, but at five o'clock on April 22 the breeze began to blow toward the Allied lines.

Chlorine, a poison, begins by irritating the eyes, nose, and throat. It quickly scorches the lining of the windpipe and the lungs, resulting in severe, often fatal, coughing bouts. In an extreme dose, such as was used that horrific day at Ypres, chlorine causes massive amounts of a yellowish fluid to develop in the lungs. Many of the men who died during or soon after the April 22 attack actually choked to death from the heavy liquid in their chests and throats.

After the Allied front had fallen silent, the Germans, wearing crude gas masks, advanced to survey the effects of the day's battle and of their new weapon. Even they were amazed at what they found. In all, more than 5,000 had died as a result of the poisonings. Over 10,000 were injured. Four miles of the Allied line had collapsed, and the gap was several miles deep. Yet the Germans, lacking sufficient reserves in that sector, were unable to capitalize on the Allies' fallen defenses. Indeed, they were not prepared for such a significant victory with their fledgling weapon,[1] or they might have marched through to the English Channel and soon attempted the capture of the French city of Calais. Had that occurred, the course of World War I might have been drastically altered.

The Germans did, however, follow up with a second

chlorine attack two days later. Again at Ypres, they were battling Canadian regiments called in to seal the gap caused by the initial gas attack. The Canadians, still without sufficient protection against the chlorine, held fabric soaked with urine to their faces in an attempt to escape the effects of the gas. The ensuing panic was similar to that of two days before, and over 5,000 Allied troops died from the combination artillery/gas attack. Still, the Germans lacked the aggressiveness to follow up on their attack, allowing the Canadian soldiers eventually to force them to retreat. These initial German poison gas attacks marked the onset of modern chemical warfare—a method that was to play a significant and devastating role during the rest of World War I.

SMOKE AND FIRE

While military experts often cite the Ypres attacks as the first uses of chemical warfare in modern times, there had been prior uses at various intervals through the ages. The earliest known forms included smoke and fire. Thousands of years before Christ, armies burned green wood to create smoke screens and to force enemies from caves and other hideouts. As early as 2000 B.C., during the wars of ancient India, soldiers used smoke screens, incendiary weapons, and toxic fumes. In 429 B.C., the Spartans employed sulfur dioxide against the Athenians during the Peloponnesian War. They burned pitch and sulfur on wood to create poisonous sulfur fumes, and they placed the torches under the city walls of Plataea. A tremendous fire and choking fumes resulted, but a sudden rainstorm is said to have drenched the fire.[2] In Spain in approximately 75 B.C. the Roman general Sertorius used an ashlike sand in the war against rebel tribesmen. The sand, according to Plutarch, caused coughing and blindness and forced the rebels to surrender within two days.

Arsenical smokes were used in China during the

Sung dynasty in approximately A.D. 1000. During medieval times, the Christians saved Belgrade from the attacking Turks by dipping rags in poison, lighting them, and fanning the fumes toward the advancing enemy.[3] The Byzantine Greeks used Greek fire, a secret chemical mixture that burst into flames when it came into contact with water. This enabled them to set fire to enemy ships at the port of Constantinople. In 1701, during the Northern War, Charles XII of Sweden created an artificial fog, enabling his army to cross the Dura River in the conflict with Russia. General Pelissier of France used smoke from green wood against the Kabyles in Ouled Ria in 1845, suffocating the entire tribe.

In 1855, during the Crimean War, the British examined enemy shells filled with cacodyl and cacodyl oxide (containing arsenic), which produced arsenical smokes after ignition. British general Dundonald suggested that sulfur dioxide be used at the siege of Sevastopol, but the British high command rejected it. They considered the effects of the chemical too horrible.[4] In 1862, during the American Civil War, Secretary of War Edwin Stanton considered a proposal to employ artillery shells filled with chlorine, but he also decided against it. During the Boer War (1899–1902), the British did use artillery shells filled with picric acid. The tactic, though controversial, was without success as the shells were extremely ineffective.

During the nineteenth and early twentieth centuries, military strategists generally considered chemical warfare to be an "indecent" and "inhumane" form of warfare. First, it caused lingering, painful deaths and horrible injuries; second, it increased the potential of civilian casualties. Until the time of the German attacks at Ypres, government and military officials had for the most part rejected chemical warfare. The Hague Treaty of 1899 outlined a prohibition that forbade "the use of projectiles the sole object of which is the diffusion of asphyxiating or deleterious gases." Signatory nations included Germany, France, Great Britain, and Russia.

The Allied forces chose to respect the treaty and did not initiate chemical warfare during World War I for several reasons. First and foremost, they feared reprisal from the enemy. Second, the Germans were advanced in chemical manufacturing, and the Allies were skeptical about their ability to match them at their own game. Finally, they considered the strength of the terms of the treaty, theorizing that the Central Powers would not choose to initiate this illegal means of warfare.[5]

Technically, however, the Germans were not the first to employ gas during the war. The French had experimented with tear gas earlier,[6] although this milder form of warfare was not considered to be in conflict with the terms of the Hague Treaty. Despite the devastation inflicted at the Battle of Ypres, the Germans argued that the release of chlorine also did not conflict with the treaty, as "projectiles" had not been used. This position infuriated the Allies and the public in general.

Prior to the initial chlorine attack, the Germans, like the French, had experimented with mild forms of riot gases. They soon considered that a stronger gas, used on a larger scale, could have a significant impact in battle, and some of the finest German chemists set to work on plans for chemical warfare. Among the chemists was future Nobel Prize winner Fritz Haber. Haber devised the plan for chlorine, readily manufactured at German plants, to be released from cylinders. The Germans were by then badly in need of an alternate form of warfare, as a naval blockade was starving them of the nitrates they needed to develop explosives. Haber's plan was quickly adopted, and Ypres was selected as the experimental site. After several months of maneuvering the cylinders into place and awaiting the appropriate weather conditions, the attack took place on April 22, 1915, and was repeated on April 24.

The Germans followed up their two April attacks at Ypres with additional chlorine attacks on May 1, 6, 10, and 24. Although casualties were still high, the Allied troops were by then equipped with stopgap preventive measures, including flannel "respirators" that were dipped in soda water, enabling them to avoid the severe effects incurred during the April attacks.

THE RACE TO RETALIATE

Allied forces, particularly the British, scrambled to respond to the German use of poison gas with similar offensive measures. The British chemical warfare effort lacked the industrial backing that the Germans had; Allied tactics had not been extensively researched and tested, and Allied soldiers had not been trained in gas warfare methods. Yet under the direction of Major Charles Howard Foulkes, appointed "gas advisor" in May 1915 by the British high command, the British army was remarkably prepared to launch a full-scale gas attack of their own five months after the first German gas campaign.

The British attack came on September 26, 1915, at Loos, Belgium. For some months the British had escaped German chemical warfare attacks, as changes in wind direction had forced the Central Powers to direct their offensive, in several formidable attacks, against the completely unprepared Russian army. At 5:50 A.M. the British released approximately 150 tons of chlorine from over 5,000 cylinders. The Germans were surprisingly unprepared for such an attack; panic ensued and the German line was broken to a depth of three miles. In all, the British captured more than 3,000 German soldiers, in addition to causing an untold number of casualties. British casualties, however, were also high in their initial attempt at gas warfare.

Not only did World War I introduce large-scale chemical warfare to the modern world, it also spurred extensive research and development in this area. The need to develop effective retaliatory measures, combined with the task of overcoming improved protective devices, escalated the improvements in chemical warfare by both sides.

Phosgene, for example, was first used by the Germans on December 19, 1915, again at Ypres. A choking gas, phosgene is several times more effective than chlorine. It causes swelling of the membranes of the respiratory tract, resulting in death by asphyxiation. Phosgene is also much more difficult to detect than chlorine. It is almost colorless and odorless, and its symptoms are usually delayed. Like chlorine, phosgene causes liquid to develop in the lungs, but over a much slower period.

In June 1916, the Allies launched their first attack with phosgene at the Battle of the Somme. A combined cloud of chlorine and phosgene was released along a 17-mile (27-km) front; it was so effective that the British carried out fifty gas attacks during the first eighteen days at the Somme. Phosgene became a primary weapon for the British chemical warfare faction.

By this time chemical warfare was being used routinely in battle. While in 1915 only 3,600 tons of gas were used, 15,000 tons were employed in 1916. The British successfully developed two new methods for the deployment of gases, putting them into use in 1917. The Livens projector—named after its inventor, Captain F. H. Livens—was a steel tube, approximately 3 to 4 feet (91 to 122 cm) long, which was buried in the ground at an angle. From the projector, 30-pound (13.6-kg) drums of chemicals were fired. The drums burst over the enemy position, releasing the gas without warning.

The Stokes mortar, also developed by the British, was a steel tube designed to fire four mortar bombs, each containing two liters of gas. The mortar provided accuracy in directing the chemicals. Both the Livens projector and the Stokes mortar were used successfully against the Germans, who had not developed such sophisticated means for delivery of poison gas.

Gas shells, logistically much simpler than heavy cylinders, were frequently used in World War I beginning in 1916. The shells, filled with chemicals and a portion of explosive, began to be manufactured and employed on a large scale, soon becoming the primary means for waging chemical warfare.

Although by 1917 chemical warfare had become a regular battlefield occurrence, refinements to protective gear enabled soldiers to combat the effects of the gas. Masks and helmets, properly used, were generally sufficient protection against chlorine and phosgene. Although gas warfare continued to be used consistently, its effects were largely negated by the improved protective devices. But in July 1917, the Germans employed mustard gas for the first time—another startling, significant step in the advancement of chemical warfare.

Dichlorodiethyl sulfide, nicknamed mustard or Yperite, is a pale yellow gas that causes severe burns to the eyes and skin and much damage to the lungs. Like phosgene, its symptoms are often delayed for hours, and it is sometimes days later that the full extent of injuries is revealed.

Mustard was an important development in chemical warfare for several reasons. First, it lessened many of the logistical problems of its predecessors. Gas cylinders, for example, were large, heavy, and difficult to transfer, maneuver, hide, and often to operate. Delivery of attack with mustard was in the form of artillery shells, and it was therefore easier to surprise the enemy. By the time troops caught unaware were able to take protective measures, mustard could already have caused extensive damage. Furthermore, the chemical affected an area— contaminating land, water, and even equipment—and rendered a site completely untenable for weeks or months, forcing troops to abandon the position. Especially important was the independence of mustard attacks from the weather: no longer did troops have to wait for select conditions to launch a chemical offensive.

The Germans introduced mustard in its brownish liquid form, encasing it in artillery shells. Again, Ypres was the site for the first attack, on July 12, 1917. Not only did the Germans launch an offensive with a severe and surprising new weapon, they employed a devastating amount of the chemical—2,500 tons within ten days. The Germans had been storing and saving the chemical for months, waiting to unleash it in amounts that would—and did—stop the enemy cold. There were nearly 15,000 reported British mustard gas casualties within three weeks.

Mustard gas quickly escalated the number of casualties related to chemical warfare in World War I. The British, for example, suffered more than 160,000 mustard casualties from July 1917 to November 1918[7]— close to 70 percent of total British gas casualties. Prior to that period they had reported 20,000 gas casualties for the two years of use. The Americans, entering the war in April 1917 and sending troops to Europe in June, suffered one-fourth of their total casualties—close to 70,000—from mustard.

Although the Allies had been familiarized with mustard gas before the Germans introduced it into the war (the British had, in fact, thought mustard too weak to merit serious consideration), it took them considerable time to get the chemical into production and to the battlefields. Not until June 1918 did the French have mustard in full-scale production; for the British, mustard did not reach military units until September 1918.

Debilitating and often lethal on the battleground, mustard was also extremely difficult and dangerous to manufacture. Overall, there was little Allied use of mustard gas before the close of the war. One incident, however, does stand out: on October 14, 1918, just before the close of the war, soldiers from the Bavarian Reserve

Infantry suffered a heavy Allied mustard attack in Werwick, Belgium. Young Adolf Hitler was among the injured.

A lack of accurate records makes it difficult to assess the exact number of World War I gas casualties, but it is estimated that there were well over a million. Over 90,000 of these were deaths. Russia suffered the most from chemical warfare with more than 400,000 casualties. Germany, France, and Britain each reported approximately 200,000. More than 100,000 tons of chemicals were used in less than four years, making chemical warfare a highly significant new weapon, along with the airplane, the tank, and the submarine.

Proponents of chemical warfare have often argued that it is a "humane" form of warfare, based on the limited number of deaths in proportion to the number of casualties. It is important to consider, however, the extensive damage the poisons inflict upon the body, and both the short- and long-term effects. Thousands lay ill for months after the initial poisonings; a large percentage suffered effects for years afterward. Many of these men later died of related illnesses such as bronchitis, tuberculosis, and cancer.

The presence of poison gas in warfare also traumatized and frightened troops. Protective gear, though necessary, was cumbersome and uncomfortable, and defensive measures were difficult. Chemical warfare introduced an unwanted, complicated, and ugly dimension to an already devastating conflict.

POSTWAR RESEARCH

Despite the abhorrence most military and government officials—as well as the public—felt for chemical warfare, its presence and impending threat were not to be ignored. There was little reason to believe that it might not be employed in a future war, and this was reflected in the broad and earnest scale with which its development was pursued after World War I had ended. The young Soviet Union, for example, suffered considerably as a result of World War I gas warfare and was thus determined to become better prepared, both offensively and defensively. Britain, France, Germany, and Italy all returned to their national chemical plants and research laboratories to further chemical developments and protective measures. Americans, too, would not soon forget the high proportion of U.S. gas casualties inflicted during the war, directing concentrated efforts toward marked progress in the field.

In the spring of 1918, shortly before the close of the war, Americans at Catholic University in Washington, D.C., discovered lewisite, a chemical as severe as mustard but with quicker action. Though lewisite never reached the battlefields, its development was an important step for the chemical warfare effort. Further studies and experiments were conducted for the United States at Edgewood Arsenal, a collective of manufacturing and weapons-filling facilities located in Edgewood, Maryland. The Edgewood plants, which began operating late in 1917, produced several chemical agents, including chlorine, phosgene, mustard, and lewisite. According to Dr. Julian Perry Robinson, in *The Rise of Chemical and Biological Weapons*, the United States was, at the time of the Armistice, "manufacturing about as much gas ... as France and the UK combined, and nearly four times as much as Germany, although little of it reached Europe in time to be used. The bulk of U.S. production came from Edgewood Arsenal."[8]

In England, research and development were conducted at Porton Down, a 7,000-acre facility opened in 1917. Britain's Holland Committee, appointed in 1919 and organized to report on chemical warfare and potential national policies, determined that "it is impossible to divorce the study of defense against gas from the study of the use of gas as an offensive weapon, as the efficiency of the defense depends entirely on an accurate knowledge as to what progress is being or is likely to be made in the offensive use of this weapon."[9]

Great Britain was also among the first to use chemical weapons after the war. Aiding the anti-Soviet armies during the Russian civil war, England supplied the "M-Device" in 1919. The system, which proved successful, consisted of the release of arsenic smoke clouds from airplanes. Also in 1919, the Royal Air Force reportedly used gas bombs, containing mustard and phosgene, against the Afghans.

In 1925 the French and Spanish used mustard gas in Morocco. This was to be the last significant employment of the gas for a few years, as the 1925 prohibition of chemical and biological warfare, known as the Geneva Protocol, did much to curtail the use of chemical weapons. There were, however, a few outstanding incidents of gas usage a few years later. In 1935 Italy invaded Ethiopia, making frequent use of poisonous chemicals. Ethiopian military casualties amounted to nearly 15,000.[10] Casualties were not, however, limited to the warring parties; numerous civilians were also killed or wounded. The Ethiopians had little protection from the chemicals, and the effects were dreadful. The Italians' use of chemical warfare was widely criticized.

The Japanese, too, employed chemical weapons in their war against the Chinese in the mid-1930s. Again, civilians were not excluded: Japanese forces often conducted mass attacks on peasants with the prohibited weapons.[11] A significant characteristic of post–World War I use of chemical weapons was that they were, for the most part, employed against unsuspecting and unprotected enemies, including civilians. Such offensives naturally proved successful, although considered cruel and unnecessary.

The greater world powers, however, were determined that they would not be caught unprepared. With the Geneva Protocol fading from memory—and prohibiting only the use of chemical weapons, not their production or stockpiling—many nations once again began to work vigorously at their chemical warfare systems. New facilities were built, and former plant operations were renewed. Chemical research, reserve buildups, and the training of military personnel in this form of warfare became top priorities.

The fear of German chemical power was behind much of this push for progress in chemical weaponry. In Europe even civilians were trained in the defense against its use. In September 1938, the British government issued millions of gas masks to its civilian population. The threat of chemical warfare had become an everyday concern.

1. Frederick J. Brown, *Chemical Warfare: A Study in Restraints*, Princeton University Press, 1968, 4.

2. Seymour M. Hersh, *Chemical and Biological Warfare: America's Hidden Arsenal* (New York: Bobbs-Merrill, 1968), 3.

3. Ibid., 4.

4. Ibid.

5. Brown, *Chemical Warfare*, 9.

6. Hersh, *Chemical and Biological Warfare*, 6.

7. Brown, *Chemical Warfare*, 12.

8. Julian Perry Robinson, *The Rise of Chemical and Biological Weapons*, Volume I, *The Problem of Chemical and Biological Warfare* (New York: Stockholm International Peace Research Institute, Humanities Press, 1971).

9. Robert Harris and Jeremy Paxman, *A Higher Form of Killing: The Secret Story of Chemical and Biological Warfare* (New York: Hill and Wang, 1982), 42.

10. Ibid., 50.

11. Ibid., 48.

HITLER'S DECISION

But for some curious twists of fate, the Nazis might have unleashed an arsenal of new, devastatingly powerful nerve gases that would have completely surprised the Allies, caused thousands—perhaps millions—of horrible deaths and injuries, and possibly have prolonged World War II for years.

One of these twists was the fact that Adolf Hitler, the fanatical leader of Nazi Germany, had himself been wounded by an attack of mustard gas during World War I. He was known to have a marked aversion to chemical weapons, and this may have contributed to his reluctance to use such weapons during World War II. The other, more important twist of fate was the inexplicable collapse of German intelligence regarding the status of the Allies' chemical warfare arsenal. By midwar the Germans had developed and were mass-producing a highly effective new nerve gas—a quantum leap beyond most of the crude mustard gases used during World War I.

A REMARKABLE DISCOVERY

The Germans more or less assumed that the Allies had developed nerve gases of equal power. The actual case was that neither the United States nor Great Britain possessed a chemical weapon even remotely capable of matching the Germans' deadly nerve gas. They would have been totally unprepared had the Nazis chosen to use such a weapon.

Hitler, however, was fearful of massive retaliation in kind if he used the nerve gas, and therefore he decided not to use it. By the time the Germans realized their potential advantage with this new weapon, it was too late in the war. They no longer had the airplanes, artillery, and rockets to deliver it effectively.

This fascinating episode in history actually began in the laboratory of the German chemist Dr. Gerhard Schrader in 1936. While searching for new insecticides at I. G. Farben, then one of the largest chemical companies in the world, Schrader accidentally made a remarkable discovery. In *A Higher Form of Killing: The Secret Story of Chemical and Biological Warfare*, Robert Harris and Jeremy Paxman describe the sequence of events:

> [Schrader] had been methodically working his way through an enormous range of organic phosphorous compounds when he suddenly stumbled upon a series of poisons of extraordinary power.
>
> On 23 December he managed to prepare some of the chemical for the first time, and tested it by spraying a concentration of just one part in 200,000 on some leaf lice. All of the insects were killed. A few weeks later, in January 1937, Schrader began the first manufacturing trials. Immediately he discovered that what he had at first considered a promising insecticide had side effects upon man which were "extremely unpleasant."[1]

According to Harris and Paxman, the first symptom Schrader noticed was that exposure to the slightest drop of the chemical in the lab caused the pupils of his eyes to contract to pinpoints and his sight to weaken noticeably in artificial light. He also suffered acute difficulty in breathing. So powerful was this new agent that he and his aides had to stop working altogether for three weeks to recover their health. As it turned out, they were "lucky to escape with their lives. Inadvertently, they had discovered, and become the victims of, the world's most powerful chemical weapon, the original 'nerve gas,' tabun."[2]

Schrader and his staff confirmed the effects of the poison—one of the deadliest and most insidious weapons ever—in subsequent tests on animals. Dogs and monkeys subjected to the nerve gas seemed to lose all muscular control. Their pupils shrank to tiny dots, and they frothed at the mouth and vomited uncontrollably. Their limbs twitched and jerked, and within ten minutes they went into violent convulsions and died.[3]

Through study Schrader learned just how tabun worked. Harris and Paxman describe the effects:

Unlike the gases of the first World War, which have a general effect, the nerve gases inhibit the action of a specific chemical in the body called cholinesterase. Cholinesterase's function is to control the muscles by breaking down acetylcholine, the chemical that causes muscular contraction. If this is not done, the level of acetylcholine in the body builds up to a disastrous level, sending all the muscles of the body into contraction. The body thus poisons itself, as it loses control of all its functions. The muscles of the arms and legs along with those which control respiration and defecation go into a state of violent vibration. Death comes as a result of asphyxiation.[4]

Schrader probably didn't realize it at the time, but his discovery was an advance in the state of chemical weaponry equivalent to the machine gun over the musket. He reported his findings to the German military command, who were impressed. They ordered construction of new laboratories and gave Schrader all the resources he needed to produce sufficient quantities of tabun for full-scale field tests.

By 1938, as Nazi Germany was gearing up for all-out war in Europe, Schrader discovered another new compound. This one—methylisopropoxy fluorophosphine oxide—was related to tabun but had a toxic substance Schrader found to be "astonishingly high."[5] It was named sarin. Initial tests on animals showed it to be almost ten times as poisonous as tabun. One-fiftieth of a drop on human skin could paralyze the nervous system within minutes, causing death soon after. Development work on both lethal nerve gases was given priority status.

Meanwhile, as the war neared, German leaders aware of the new weapons in the works began advocating their use. In 1939, Hermann Ochsner, the general in command of all German chemical troops, called for the use of gas "against industrial concentrations and large cities" as a weapon of terror. "There is no doubt," he said, "that a city like London would be plunged into a state of unbearable turmoil which would bring enormous pressure to bear on the enemy government."

Hitler also apparently was considering the awesome potential of the nerve gases. On September 19, 1939, three weeks after he had launched the invasion of Poland, he referred in a speech to "fearsome new German weapons, against which the enemy would be defenseless."

Four months later, construction of a new factory for the production of tabun was begun at a place called Dyhernfurth in the forests of Silesia in western Poland. It was to have a capacity of 3,000 tons of nerve gas a month, as well as a facility for loading the gas into aircraft bombs and shells.

There were problems from the start, however. The new chemical was so corrosive, for example, that all steel and iron equipment in the plant had to be silver-plated. And it was so toxic that it caused hundreds of accidents that killed and injured scores of workers. In one recorded instance some tabun leaked onto four workmen cleaning pipes. They died in convulsions before their protective rubber suits could be stripped from them.[6]

It took over two years to get Dyhernfurth operational. All during this time the Allies had no idea the Germans were even working on a new chemical weapon, much less mass-producing one. It was one of the best-kept secrets of the war, rivaling even the great secrecy that later shrouded the development of the atomic bomb in the United States. Even the German scientists working on the project knew only of the small part with which they were involved.

The secret held for eight years. Early Allied intelligence reports had referred to the development of secret weapons thought to be of a chemical nature, but apparently these were either not believed or were disregarded. Only in April 1945, a few weeks before the end of the war in Europe, did the Allies learn about the new nerve gases. This happened when a German ammunition dump was captured and a "mysterious shell" was shipped back to England for examination by chemical experts. They were astounded at what they found.

HITLER'S FEAR OF RETALIATION

By the middle of 1943, as the tide of war began to change in favor of the Allies, Hitler began to seriously consider using nerve gases. By this time the Germans had acquired a vast secret stockpile of chemical weapons. Enormous amounts of money and armies of top scientific talent had been pumped into the project. No expense had been spared, and buildings and equipment had been provided on a lavish scale.

Several factories had been erected, and the Germans now had the capacity to produce 12,000 tons of poison gas a month. Estimates vary on how much gas the Germans had stockpiled, ranging from 70,000 to 250,000 tons. This included tabun and at least two types of mustard gas.[7] Sarin also was entering the production phase, and development work was under way on soman, the deadliest of all nerve gases at that time.

Additionally, considerable work had gone into delivery systems for the gases. Gases were implanted in land mines. Hand grenades were filled with poisonous solutions. Hand sprays were perfected. Artillery shells were filled with gas. Aircraft sprays were developed. It is estimated that the Luftwaffe, the German air force, had almost half a million gas bombs in inventory. From inside Germany, enormous pressure was exerted on Hitler to launch the new weapons. Three of the most fanatical Nazi leaders—Martin Bormann, Hermann Goering, and Robert Ley—repeatedly urged Hitler to take such action. There is evidence that the German führer seriously considered it. He spoke of using gas against the Russians on the eastern front, believing the United States and other Allied nations would not object too strenuously because they also feared the Russians.

There is also speculation that Hitler thought of loading V-1 and V-2 rockets with lethal concentrations of gas to explode on millions of Londoners. In June 1944, he boasted to the Italian leader Benito Mussolini of secret weapons that would "turn London into a garden of ruins," and he specifically referred to a deadly new gas being developed by German scientists.

In fact, the Germans made plans to deliver nerve gases to the very heart of London via the V series of rockets. It was estimated that waves of 200 rockets a day could be launched over the English coast.

Even at this point it is speculative if a decision by Hitler to use nerve gas might have dramatically altered the outcome of the war. Although Allied military experts agree that had gases been used on the troops invading the Normandy beaches on June 6, 1944, the successful D-Day landings would have been turned into a disaster, they contend that Allied retaliation efforts, which might have included the use of the atomic bomb, would have soon spelled catastrophe for the Germans.

Hitler, however, procrastinated. To some extent his intelligence services let him down. He was fearful that if he used tabun and the other gases, the Allies would bomb German cities with gases of their own, killing and maiming tens or hundreds of thousands of German civilians and contaminating the countryside perhaps for years to come. Indeed, the Allies were capable of launching devastating air attacks with both chemical and biological agents, but they did not possess the advanced chemical weapons Hitler and his advisers suspected.

Interestingly enough, at one point in the war when things looked bad for Great Britain as V-1 rockets threatened London, the British were considering using poison gas on the Germans. Prime Minister Winston Churchill wrote in a memo to his service chiefs:

> I want you to think very seriously over this question of poison gas. I would not use it unless it could be shown either that it was life or death for us, or that it would shorten the war by a year.
>
> It is absurd to consider morality on this topic when everybody used it in the last war without a word of complaint from the moralists or the church. On the other hand, in the last war the bombing of open cities was regarded as forbidden. Now everybody does it as a matter of course. It is simply a question of fashion changing as she does between long and short skirts for women.
>
> I want a cold-blooded calculation as to how it would pay us to use poison gas. . . . If the bombardment of London really became a serious nui-

36

sance and great rockets with far-reaching and devastating effect fall on many centers of government
and labor, I should be prepared to do anything that
would hit the enemy in a murderous place.

I may certainly have to ask you to support me
in using poison gas. We could drench the cities of
the Ruhr and many other cities in Germany in such
a way that most of the population could be requiring constant medical attention. . . . I do not see
why we should always have all the disadvantages
of being the gentlemen while they [the Germans]
have all the advantages of being the cad.[8]

Perhaps luckily for Britain and the Allies, Churchill never
had to ask his chiefs' support for use of the gas, for had
the British used it Hitler surely would have countered
with his far more lethal chemical arsenal. Still, it is estimated that several thousand British scientists, technicians, and others were involved in poison gas research,
development, and manufacture during the war.

With one notable exception, the United States never
seriously considered using gas during World War II. President Franklin D. Roosevelt was vehemently opposed to
it. He said in 1943: "Use of such weapons [chemical and
biological] has been outlawed by the general opinion of
civilized mankind. This country has not used them. I
state categorically that we shall under no circumstances
resort to the use of such weapons unless they are first
used by our enemies."[9]

Despite his hatred of CBW, Roosevelt authorized the
buildup of American stockpiles of gas weapons during
the war, in part because of a widespread belief that the
Japanese might launch poison gas attacks in the Pacific
fighting. And it was in the Pacific theater that the United
States thought of using gas. The American high command recommended saturating the island of Iwo Jima
with gas in 1944 just before the Allied landing there.

Japanese troops were fortified in tunnels and caves, and U.S. military commanders argued that gas would flush them out and thus reduce American casualties during the invasion. Roosevelt flatly turned down the proposal, but at a cost. Some of the heaviest fighting in the Pacific occurred on Iwo Jima. Nearly 7,000 Americans lost their lives, and there were almost 25,000 casualties.

There also was some thought given to using poison gas if Japan itself had to be invaded, but any such plans were canceled with the development of the atomic bomb and its use on Hiroshima and Nagasaki.

By 1945 it was too late for Hitler. Even if he had ordered a gas attack, he no longer had sufficient means to deliver it. His once proud Luftwaffe had been decimated. There no longer were enough planes left to bomb the Allies with gas, nor were there enough rockets. Nazi factories and development centers had been bombed into submission.

Top German leaders under Hitler knew this, and had he, as a last-ditch attempt of a madman, still demanded an attack of gas weapons, they were prepared to ignore the orders. They knew by then it would be suicidal.

Most historians contend that even if tabun and the other nerve gases had been launched, they would not have affected the eventual Allied victory; they would only have prolonged the war, causing even greater casualties on both sides. The real fear, they argue, was of massive gas attacks on European cities, which would have killed great numbers of civilians and left a long-lingering pall of devastation over the metropolitan areas.

But others believe that if Hitler had realized his advantage and chosen to use the nerve gases shortly after initial production began—early in the war—this might well have altered the outcome of World War II.

At the end of the war, twenty old merchant vessels, loaded with tens of thousands of tons of captured German gas, were sunk in deep waters off the coast of Norway.

1. Robert Harris and Jeremy Paxman, *A Higher Form of Killing: The Secret Story of Chemical and Biological Warfare* (New York: Hill and Wang, 1982), 53.

2. Ibid.

3. Ibid.

4. Ibid., 54.

5. Ibid.

6. Ibid., 57.

7. Ibid., 58.

8. Public Record Office, London, July 6, 1944.

9. Richard D. McCarthy, *The Ultimate Folly* (New York: Alfred A. Knopf, 1990), 9.

PLAGUE AND PESTILENCE

Six hundred years before the birth of Christ, the soldiers of Kirrha, locked in battle with the troops of Solon of Athens, mysteriously became ill. Many died and others, too sick to fight, became easy prey for the enemy. Their drinking water had been poisoned with the rotting carcasses of animals. Solon won the conflict by what may have been the first use of biological weapons.

In the fourteenth century, it is reported that the Tartars captured the Crimean town of Kaffa by catapulting bodies of plague victims into the walled city.[1] In North America in the eighteenth century, British military leaders sent blankets bearing smallpox germs to Indian camps in hopes of spreading the dread disease. The ploy worked, causing epidemic in some areas.[2]

While there is no recorded use of disease as a weapon in modern times, there were allegations of attempted use during World War I. The Germans were accused of inoculating horses and mules with glanders, a highly infectious animal disease. They were also charged with infecting cattle with anthrax. An acutely infectious and deadly disease that generally occurs in sheep or cattle, anthrax can be equally deadly to humans. In a matter of hours, the tiniest of doses can produce a choking cough, difficulty in breathing, and a high fever. In most cases, death follows.

There were also reports that German spies were caught trying to spread dreaded plague bacteria in Russia in 1915 and 1916. Plague, the notorious Black Death that killed hundreds of thousands of Europeans during an outbreak centuries ago, is extremely contagious, and untreated patients normally die within two or three days.

CULTIVATING CALAMITY: GERM WARFARE RESEARCH

The thought of using germs and disease as weapons is so abhorrent to the general public that their use has been generally nonexistent in the twentieth century. Still, the marching advance of scientific technology, especially in the fields of medicine and chemistry, has given rise to fears of new biological weapons in time of war. In fact, several nations have worked on the development of such weapons over the past fifty years, and arsenals of deadly germs are a reality to this day.

As early as 1925, Winston Churchill wrote of the fearsome potential of biological warfare: "Pestilences methodically prepared and deliberately launched upon man and beast . . . blight to destroy crops . . . anthrax to slay horses and cattle . . . plague to poison not armies but whole districts . . . such are the lines along which military science is remorselessly advancing."[3]

Use of biological weapons was outlawed under the terms of the 1925 Geneva Protocol. Nevertheless, in the years leading up to World War II and during the war itself, many nations developed such weapons. Japan was one of the first countries to do this.

Japanese research in this field began in the mid-1930s. In 1937 Japan built the first known major biological warfare installation in the world. Here extensive research was conducted on such diseases as typhus, typhoid, anthrax, cholera, plague, salmonella, tetanus, botulism, brucellosis, gas gangrene, smallpox, tick encephalitis, tuberculosis, tularemia, and glanders.

Anthrax was tested extensively as a bomb filling. The Japanese worked for at least seven years on this project. They also tested germ-filled artillery shells, aerial sprays, and sabotage devices for poisoning water supplies. A single wound from a piece of anthrax-contaminated shrapnel was estimated to cause illness and death in 90 percent of victims.

Experiments also were conducted with sabotage techniques for contaminating foodstuffs. One contaminant was made of an extract from the poisonous livers of blowfish. The Japanese also cultivated the plague-infested flea as a weapon, and at one time built up a capacity to produce 500 million such fleas a year.

It is now believed by U.S. intelligence agencies that the Japanese infected thousands of human prisoners, mostly Chinese, with disease-bearing germs in insidious experiments in the late 1930s and early 1940s. Prisoners were infected with tetanus, smallpox, plague, and glanders, and bombs of anthrax were exploded amid groups of human guinea pigs. There are reports that thousands of soldiers died of cholera, and in one instance 2,000 horses were killed by anthrax.

There also is evidence to suggest that the Japanese actually used biological weapons in their fighting against the Chinese. Spies are said to have carried biological agents in ampules for sabotage missions behind enemy lines. In 1940, historical documents indicate, Japanese planes scattered rice and wheat grains mixed with infested fleas over Chuhsien and other Chinese towns. Scores of peasants subsequently died of the plague, and thousands of acres of rice paddies were destroyed.[4]

The entire Japanese biological weapon development

operation was kept under the tightest secrecy. Although at one time there were about eighteen biological warfare "out stations," each manned by 300 or more workers, little word of what was going on seeped to the outside world. Even the Japanese emperor was not informed, and the full story of this large-scale effort was not fully revealed until a quarter of a century after World War II.

As war drew closer in the late 1930s, there was great fear, especially among the British and the Americans, that the Axis powers might launch massive biological attacks, against which no adequate defense could be prepared. These attacks would have one simple aim: to wipe out such a huge proportion of the enemy's population, civilians and military alike, that the nation's whole war machine would cease to function.

The only way to counter such a threat, it was believed, was to develop an arsenal of biological weapons that could be launched in retaliation. Thus, both Britain and the United States poured millions of dollars and thousands of skilled workers into the project.

The British, like the Japanese, did considerable work on the development of anthrax as a major weapon. In 1942 teams of British scientists went to the isolated island of Gruinard, off the northwest coast of Scotland. There, shrouded in secrecy, they set up field tests of a bomb containing concentrated anthrax spores.

When the bomb was set off, billions of spores formed an invisible cloud that wafted over the thousands of sheep on the island. A day later the sheep began to die, thus proving that biological warfare was not only a nightmarish concept but a grim reality. As a result of the experiments, Gruinard remains uninhabitable today.

Not only did the experiment prove that the organisms could survive the explosion on the island, anthrax contamination also began to surface on the Scottish mainland, despite the scientists' precautions. "Whether the mainland infections were caused by unexpected winds or by an infected carcass that floated downstream remains uncertain," writes Leonard A. Cole in *Clouds of Secrecy: The Army's Germ Warfare Tests Over Populated Areas*, "but the incident was viewed as a crisis at Porton Down, Britain's chemical and biological warfare center."[5]

Later, the British began to manufacture 4-pound (1.8-kg) anthrax bombs. These were loaded, 106 at a time, into 500-pound (227-kg) cluster bombs. On detonation such weapons would disperse the anthrax spores over great areas, killing an estimated half of the population exposed to them by inhalation. More would die from skin contamination. Terrain saturated with anthrax would remain contaminated for years afterward. At the time there was no known method of decontamination and no preventive inoculation.

Recently declassified government papers indicate that the British gave serious consideration to using anthrax bombs on German cities. According to Stanford University historian Barton J. Bernstein, the British refrained from such an attack because other Allied initiatives were proving successful, and because they feared retaliation in kind by the Germans.[6]

The Germans did not consider biological weapons seriously until July 1943. Then, at a secret conference of the Nazi high command, it was decided that an institute should be created for the production of bacterial cultures on a large scale, and experiments should be conducted to examine the possibilities of using bacteria in the war. There is evidence that hideous experiments were undertaken on prisoners in concentration camps at Dachau, Natzweiler, and Buchenwald. In some instances inmates were deliberately covered with typhus-infected lice. The project never got very far. In two years the Germans were not able to produce a feasible weapon, and by that time the war was nearly over.

U.S. interest in biological warfare was spurred in August 1941, only months before America entered the war. Military officials feared a biological attack, and, according to Cole, "Secretary of War Henry Stimson asked the National Academy of Sciences to evaluate the subject, and a committee appointed by the academy concluded that biological warfare was feasible."[7] Following President Roosevelt's approval in 1942, a Special Assignments branch was formed at the Edgewood Chemical Arsenal in Maryland. More than $40 million was spent on the plant and equipment during the war years, and 4,000 people were involved in biological warfare research, testing, and production.

Such potential weapons as anthrax, glanders, brucellosis, tularemia, meliodosis, plague, typhus, psittacosis, yellow fever, encephalitis, fowl pest, rinder pest, and various food blights were investigated. Entomological warfare teams experimented with Colorado beetles, fleas, and other insects for use as possible weapons. Much work was done on developing anticrop germ agents.

With technological help from Britain, the United States developed the capability to launch a potentially catastrophic attack on enemy food supplies. Again, it was a top-secret effort. By 1944, the United States had the capacity to produce 50,000 anthrax bombs a month.

Near the war's end, the United States was working on development of a weapon designed to spread brucellosis. This disease, although rarely fatal, is extremely debilitating, causing chills, fever, headache, loss of appetite, mental depression, extreme exhaustion, aching joints, and sweating. Highly infectious, it was estimated to be capable of putting a soldier out of action for up to a year.

By the end of World War II, the United States and Britain each had massive hidden arsenals of anticrop sprays and germ weapons. Fortunately, biological weapons were never used during the war.

THE TOP-SECRET PURSUIT

During the years between the end of World War II (1945) and 1969, when President Richard Nixon called for a halt to biological weapons, it is estimated that the United States spent more than $700 million on development of so-called germ warfare. This included continuing work on plague, anthrax, tularemia, psittacosis, Q fever, botulism, Rocky Mountain spotted fever, brucellosis, and Venezuelan equine encephalitis.

Much of this work was done at the Pine Bluff Arsenal Research and Development Center near Little Rock, Arkansas. Here, in 1964, for example, the army spent $25 million to expand the top-secret $79 million biological warfare production facilities in the north area of the arsenal. Cold-storage igloos contained stockpiles of anthrax, tularemia, and Venezuelan equine encephalitis.

On the East Coast, at Fort Detrick, near historic Frederick, Maryland, the army maintained another biological weapon developing facility. Military officials said the main purpose of the effort there was to develop vaccines for use in combating diseases. Dogs, monkeys, mice, guinea pigs, hamsters, and human beings were used in tests at the site. An estimated $20 million a year was spent on producing such diseases as pneumonic plague and pulmonary anthrax, as well as botulism toxin. It was reported that just one ounce of this toxin, effectively dispersed, was enough to kill every man, woman, and child in North America.

The work at Fort Detrick was dangerous. Several deaths were caused by worker exposure to the deadly biological agents, and there were hundreds of cases of serious illness.

Congressman Richard D. McCarthy of New York said the United States twice came close to using biological warfare against Cuba in 1962. One plan apparently called for destruction of the Cuban sugar crop with a biological agent. Another was designed to drop germs over the island to infect people with an incapacitating agent. Both plans were scrapped.

As research and development of bacteria were being conducted, the military also plotted ways to use such germs in time of war. In one bizarre incident, for example, the army, in a mock raid in 1966, "attacked" New York City by spreading harmless bacteria throughout the city's massive subway system. Officials found such attacks terrifyingly simple, showing this nation's vulnerability to germ warfare. Whole cities could be paralyzed.[8]

In reality, there is no viable defense for civilian populations against germ attack. There is not even a meaningful warning system. No one would know there had been an assault until people began to get sick and die. In 1969 the Department of State said on this point:

> The U.S. does not maintain large stockpiles of medical supplies such as antibiotics and vaccines against the possibility of biological attack. There is no specific antibiotic therapy available for most biological warfare agents. As for vaccines, there are more than 100 possible biological warfare agents, and production and administration of 100 vaccines to the U.S. population is not practical. There is medical reason to believe that such a program would be generally injurious to health in addition to requiring prohibitive expenditures.

THE SEED OF DESTRUCTION

Proponents of biological weapons say their use could actually save lives during a war. Said General J. H. Rothschild, former head of the U.S. Army's Chemical Corps: "Suppose the enemy conspired to start a so-called 'limited war' in another country—a possibility which seems much more likely than the outbreak of an all-out war. We would want to cause the smallest amount of suffering to the people of the disrupted nation, and again, chemical and biological agents could be used to incapacitate rather than kill."

But critics say such a philosophy would be extremely dangerous, especially with biological weapons. "We don't know what would happen," said Congressman McCarthy. "We don't understand the effects. Civilians probably would be slaughtered." What might start out as an "incapacitating agent," critics contend, could become highly lethal and spread around the world as an epidemic.

Still, despite these dangers there remains great fear that biological weapons will be used, and possibly not by a world power but by a developing country or terrorist group. This is because such weapons are relatively inexpensive to produce. According to a United Nations report: "The possibility always exists that by choosing a single agent and a simple means of delivery, a nation could equip itself relatively cheaply to attack a limited area with a reasonable chance of success."

"The specter of chemical and biological warfare arouses horror and revulsion throughout the world," President Nixon said in 1969. "Mankind already carries in its own hands too many of the seeds of its own destruction. The United States shall renounce the use of lethal biological agents and weapons and all other methods of biological warfare."

Three years later, on April 4, 1972, representatives of the United States and the Soviet Union signed an agreement that stated they would "never in any circumstances, develop, produce, stockpile, or otherwise acquire or retain" any biological weapons. More than 100 countries have signed this agreement, which does permit defensive research such as the development of vaccines and biological agents used to test protective gear and equipment.

This, it was thought at the time, effectively ended the biological weapons race. But did it? In subsequent years, there were a number of reports indicating that the Soviets continued their research and development in this area. A *San Francisco Chronicle* article, for instance, reported: "The Soviet Union is mass-producing enormous quantities of disease agents for aggressive use against the soldiers and civilians of the free world. In particular, the Red Army is stockpiling two specific 'biological weapons' with which it expects to strike a strategic blow and win any future war decisively even before it gets started officially."[9]

In 1979, a major incident at Sverdlovsk in the Soviet Union again raised questions about Soviet compliance with the prohibition on production of biological weapons. Here a sudden, major anthrax outbreak occurred near a suspected biological weapons facility. Hundreds of civilians either died or became seriously ill.

A U.S. congressional hearing on the disaster found that "an explosion at military compound 19 in Sverdlovsk released a cloud of anthrax spores into the atmosphere. . . . Winds blew the anthrax cloud south, starting from the location of compound 19 at the town's outskirts. Although as many as 1,000 residents of the suburbs may have perished, the epidemic was less severe than if the winds had been blowing toward the center of town. Soviet authorities conducted repeated vaccinations of the populace, explaining at first that nothing was wrong, and later that a 'mistake' had occurred." According to another report, despite rushed vaccinations, "about 30 to 40 people died each day and this went on for a month."[10]

Many scientists and weapons analysts remain unconvinced, however, by the U.S. interpretation of the Sverdlovsk incident. The Soviets claimed that the outbreak was the result of tainted meat, which then led to numerous incidences of gastric anthrax, as opposed to respiratory—or pulmonary—anthrax infection. Their story is supported in part by the documented prevalence of anthrax outbreaks in that region over the years. Further, analysts argue, the cloud of spores that would have resulted from an explosion would have dissipated quickly, making it unlikely that reports of pulmonary anthrax would have continued for as long as a month.[11]

While the Sverdlovsk incident continues to be debated, the severity of the tragedy underscores the lethal, and often uncontrollable, threat of anthrax poisoning and of biological warfare in general. The Biological Weapons Convention continues to be reviewed in order to further limit biological warfare activities within the scope of defense and detection efforts and to strengthen enforcement, but some analysts are concerned about the treaty's effectiveness in light of continued research and development in biotechnology.

Further, several nations, including ten in or near the Middle East, are not parties to the Biological Weapons Convention. "For a time, universal adherence seemed possible to achieve," notes Susan Wright, editor of *Preventing a Biological Arms Race*, adding that, "All known stockpiles of biological and toxin weapons were destroyed in the 1970s. . . . But the prospects for maintaining a worldwide ban on biological weapons appear less hopeful today."[12] The United States continues to closely watch the suspected activities of nations such as Iraq, which finally admitted in August 1991 that its Salman Park complex, just south of Baghdad, contained a "laboratory for biological research for military purposes."[13] Meanwhile, effective U.S. defense measures continue to be researched.

The United States, according to Reginald Bartholomew, under secretary for Security Assistance, Science and Technology, is "especially concerned about the spread of biological weapons in unstable areas," as well as the prospects of biological and toxin weapons falling into the hands of terrorists or into the arsenals of those states

50

which actively support terrorist organizations . . . we cannot dismiss these possibilities. If the proliferation of biological weapons continues, it may be only a matter of time before terrorists do acquire and use these weapons."[14]

Renewing a biological arms race would prove catastrophic. With today's technology, humans have the capability of developing and delivering great clouds of germs that not only would kill or incapacitate all living things they are dispersed upon, but also would render great areas of the earth uninhabitable, perhaps for generations.

1. Vincent J. Derbes, "De Mussis and the Great Plague of 1348," *Journal of the American Medical Association* 196, no. 1 (April 1966).

2. E. Wagner Stearn and Allen E. Stearn, *The Effect of Smallpox on the Destiny of the Amerindian* (Boston: Bruce Humphries Publishers, 1945), 44–55.

3. Winston Churchill, *The Gathering Storm* (London, 1948), 34.

4. John W. Powell, "A Hidden Chapter in History," *Bulletin of the Atomic Scientists*, October 1981, 43–52.

5. Leonard A. Cole, *Clouds of Secrecy: The Army's Germ Warfare Tests Over Populated Areas* (Totowa, N.J.: Rowman & Littlefield, 1988), 25. See also Gwynne Roberts, "The Deadly Legacy of Anthrax Island," (*London*) *Times Magazine*, Sunday, 15 February 1981, 25.

6. Barton J. Bernstein, *Bulletin of the Atomic Scientists*, January/February 1987.

7. Cole, *Clouds of Secrecy*, 14.

8. Ibid., 59–71. See also Department of the Army, "A Study of the Vulnerability of Subway Passengers in New York City to Covert Action with Biological Agents," Misc. Pub., 25 January 1968.

9. *San Francisco Examiner*, 2 June 1952.

10. House Subcommittee on Oversight, Permanent Select Committee on Intelligence, *The Sverdlovsk Incident:*

Soviet Compliance with the Biological Weapons Convention?, 29 May 1980.

11. Thomas Whiteside, "Annals of the Cold War (Chemical and Biological Warfare), Part II," *New Yorker*, 18 February 1991, 60. See also Elisa D. Harris, "Sverdlovsk and Yellow Rain: Two Cases of Soviet Noncompliance?" *International Security*, Spring 1987, 52, and Nicholas Wade, "Death at Sverdlovsk: A Critical Diagnosis," *Science*, 26 September 1980, 1501–2.

12. Susan Wright, "Biowar Treaty in Danger," *Bulletin of the Atomic Scientists*, September 1991, 36.

13. R. Jeffrey Smith, "Iraq Admits to Germ Warfare Research," *Washington Post*, August 6, 1991.

14. Reginald Bartholomew, "U.S. Efforts Against the Spread of Chemical Weapons," Department of State, Bureau of Public Affairs, 22 June 1989.

THE YELLOW RAIN CONTROVERSY

No episode in the history of modern chemical and biological warfare has been more controversial, confusing, and potentially explosive in its impact on the superpowers' relationship during the Cold War era than the period of suspected Soviet-sponsored poison gas attacks in Afghanistan, Laos, and Kampuchea (Cambodia) from 1975 through 1984. A blistering Reagan administration report issued by Secretary of State Alexander Haig in March 1982 pointed to "compelling evidence that tens of thousands of unsophisticated and defenseless peoples" had been subjected to "a campaign of chemical attacks."

A "GENOCIDAL CAMPAIGN"

The accusations led to bitter confrontations between the United States and the Soviet Union over the alleged infractions, which, the U.S. claimed, had resulted in more than 10,000 deaths by 1981.[1] Ultimately, the Pentagon's concern over the Soviet role in the poison gas attacks and its suspicion that the U.S.S.R. had been building up its

CBW arsenals and capabilities became critical factors in the decision in 1985 to renew production of nerve gas weapons after the moratorium imposed by President Nixon in 1969.

The heart of the controversy lay in reported use of mycotoxins (a toxic substance produced by a fungus) against anticommunist rebels in Southeast Asia and Afghanistan. Evidence consisted of interviews with victims and eyewitnesses; samples of vegetation carrying the suspected contaminants (soon dubbed "yellow rain" because the victims' testimony often described "showers" of a yellow, powdery substance); and the testimony of doctors, journalists, and others who examined and/or questioned the victims and eyewitnesses. A report issued by Secretary of State George Shultz in November 1982 described a typical account: "Usually the Hmong state that aircraft or helicopters spray a yellow rain-like material on their villages and crops. . . . We now know that the yellow rain contains trichothecene toxins and other substances that cause victims to experience vomiting, bleeding, blistering, severe skin lesions and other lingering signs and symptoms."[2]

Among the earliest reports to the U.S. was a telegram from the U.S. embassy in Bangkok, Thailand, to Washington in September 1978. It described interviews with Hmong refugees who "claimed to have been attacked by aircraft with rockets, bombs, stones, and 'medicine from the sky.' "[3] The following month, United Press International quoted one of the Hmong tribesmen as saying that his village had been devastated by rocket attacks that produced clouds of red, green, yellow, and white gas. "The people who sniffed the gas spun around, fainted and later died," he said. "They vomited very much. . . . Every time they used the gas rockets at least fifteen to twenty people were killed. I have never seen anything like it. All the animals in the vicinity were killed. The gas poisoned the water. We could find no shelter from it."[4]

Secretary Haig stated in his report to Congress that over 200 such attacks had been cited in Laos, more than 100 in Kampuchea, and nearly 50 in Afghanistan. "Over the past seven years chemical and toxin weapons have been used, on an ever-widening scale, in genocidal campaigns against defenseless people. These weapons are being used for precisely the reason mankind has condemned and sought to destroy them—because of their indiscriminate action and horrific effects. Today evidence of chemical and toxin warfare has accumulated to the point where the international community can no longer ignore the challenge."[5]

In his address, Haig said the report was "drawn from information made available to the United States Government since 1975. It contains the most comprehensive compilation of material on this subject available, and presents conclusions which are fully shared by all relevant agencies of the United States Government."[6] He added that the report was based on a massive amount of information, from a variety of sources, which had been carefully collected and analyzed over the years. The evidence was based largely on

- Testimony of those who saw, experienced, and suffered from chemical weapons attacks
- Testimony of doctors, refugee workers, journalists, and others who had the opportunity to question large numbers of those with firsthand experience of chemical warfare
- Testimony of those who engaged in chemical weapons attacks or were in a position to observe those who did
- Scientific evidence, based on the analysis of physical samples taken from sites where attacks had been conducted

- Documentary evidence from open sources
- Intelligence derived from "national technical means"[7]

"Taken together," the Haig report continued, "this evidence has led the U.S. Government to conclude that Lao and Vietnamese forces, operating under Soviet supervision, have, since 1975, employed lethal chemical and toxin weapons in Laos; that Vietnamese forces have, since 1978, used lethal chemical and toxin agents in Kampuchea; and that Soviet forces have used a variety of lethal chemical warfare agents, including nerve gases, in Afghanistan since the Soviet invasion of that country in 1979."[8]

Haig's report included the following descriptions of the alleged attacks:

Laos. "The U.S. Government has concluded from all the evidence that selected Lao and Vietnamese forces, under direct Soviet supervision, have employed lethal trichothecene toxins and other combinations of chemical agents against Hmong resisting government control and their villages since at least 1976. Trichothecene toxins have been positively identified, but medical symptoms indicate that irritants, incapacitants, and nerve agents also have been employed. Thousands have been killed or severely injured. Thousands also have been driven from their homeland by the use of these agents."[9]

Reports collected by the State Department describe more than 260 separate attacks in Laos during a seven-year period from 1975 to 1982. Over 6,500 deaths and thousands of serious injuries were cited as having resulted directly from exposure to chemical agents.

Kampuchea. "Vietnamese forces have used lethal trichothecene toxins on Democratic Kampuchean troops and Khmer villages since at least 1978. Medical evidence indicates that irritants, incapacitants, and nerve agents also have been used."[10]

Eyewitness accounts said the chemicals used were green and yellow, and powderlike in appearance. In some instances, the gas was described as yellow or white. Symptoms of victims coated with these substances included "tightening of the chest, disorientation, vomiting, bleeding from the nose and gums, discoloration of the body, and 'stiffening' of the teeth." In one account, artillery attacks produced "a black smoke causing itchy skin, weakness, skin lesions, and in some cases decaying skin and blisters."[11]

Afghanistan. "Soviet forces in Afghanistan have used a variety of lethal and nonlethal chemical agents on Mujahedin resistance forces and Afghan villages since the Soviet invasion in December 1979. In addition, there is some evidence that Afghan government forces may have used Soviet-supplied chemical weapons against the Mujahedin even before the Soviet invasion.

"Although it has not been possible to verify through sample analysis the specific agents used by the Soviets, a number of Afghan military defectors have named the agents brought into the country by the Soviets and have described where and when they were employed. This information has been correlated with other evidence, including the reported symptoms, leading to the conclusion that nerve agents, phosgene oxime, and various incapacitants and irritants have been used. Other agents and toxic smokes also are in the country. Some reported symptoms are consistent with those produced by lethal or sublethal doses of trichothecene toxins, but this evidence is not conclusive."[12]

For the period spanning the summer of 1979 to the summer of 1982, the U.S. government received accounts of forty-seven separate chemical attacks in Afghanistan.

There was an estimated death toll of over 3,000 people. Reports indicated that fixed-wing aircraft and helicopters were employed to disseminate chemical warfare agents by rockets, bombs, and sprays. Chemical-filled land mines were also reportedly used by the Soviets. The chemical clouds were usually gray or blue-black, yellow, or a combination of colors.[13]

The alleged chemical use in Afghanistan was said to have caused some unusual aftereffects. There were reports that some victims' bodies were characterized by abnormal bloating and blackened skin with a dark-reddish tinge. The flesh appeared decayed very soon after death. In one instance, three dead Mujahedin guerrillas were found with "hands on rifles and lying in a firing position, indicating that the attacker had used an extremely rapid-acting lethal chemical that is not detectable by normal senses and that causes no outward physiological responses before death."[14]

THE SOVIET CONNECTION

The conclusion is inescapable, Haig's report states, "that the toxins and other chemical warfare agents were developed in the Soviet Union, provided to the Lao and Vietnamese either directly or through the transfer of know-how, and weaponized with Soviet assistance in Laos, Vietnam, and Kampuchea."

> Soviet military forces are known to store agents in bulk and move them to the field for munitions fill as needed. This practice also is followed in Southeast Asia and Afghanistan, as evidenced by many reports which specify that Soviet technicians supervise the shipment, storage, filling, and loading onto aircraft of the chemical munitions.
>
> The dissemination techniques reported and observed evidently have been drawn from years of

Soviet chemical warfare testing and experimentation. There is no evidence to support any alternative explanation, such as the hypothesis that the Vietnamese produce and employ toxin weapons completely on their own. . . . Initially, there was a tendency to interpret the Soviet role as strictly advisory. Now, however, there is considerable evidence to suggest that the Soviets are far more involved in the Lao and Vietnamese chemical warfare program than was assumed earlier.[15]

THE BEE POLLEN THEORY

On a hot, humid day in the Malaysian jungle, we were observing a colony of giant Asiatic honeybees, Apis dorsata, *nested beneath a tree branch. The thirty to fifty thousand bees hanging from the comb were arranged in neat rows that formed a curtain over the nest. Suddenly the entire colony took flight. The swarm flew from the tree in a gentle arc and returned a few minutes later—after spattering everything below with tiny yellow spots.*[16]

While the Reagan administration was confident that it had built a substantial case for Soviet violation of the Geneva Protocol, based on the samples collected from the region and the testimony of victims and witnesses, many scientists and analysts remained hesitant. Several criticized the data collection process and voiced their skepticism over the laboratory results that indicated the presence of mycotoxins. They were further unconvinced that the toxins could not necessarily be found naturally in the region of Southeast Asia.

"To accuse the Russians of using Southeast Asia as a testbed for an arsenal of novel chemical weapons requires a higher standard of proof," commented science writer Nicholas Wade. "[The government] has gone public with a sketchily documented case, as if the desire to bespatter the Russians has outweighed a judgment to wait for a firmer case. The State Department is right to be concerned about the presence of novel toxins in the samples it has collected. The evidence already in hand is sufficient to suggest that a serious investigation of yellow rain should begin."[17]

Dr. Matthew Meselson, a professor of biochemistry at Harvard, urged that the administration proceed carefully with analysis of the findings. In late 1981, before the U.S. claims became widely publicized through Secretary of State Haig's special report, Meselson counseled, "I would recommend caution in concluding whether or not trichothecene mycotoxins have been used in Southeast Asia, although I agree that the preliminary evidence indicates that they have. We know very little about the normal occurrence of trichothecene mycotoxins in the tropics . . . we should avoid hasty assertions that the trichothecenes detected in Southeast Asia cannot be of normal occurrence."[18]

The most damaging discovery to the U.S. position was the determination in early 1982 that the samples collected—specifically, the so-called yellow rain—consisted almost entirely of pollen. First discovered by British scientists at the Chemical Defense Establishment at Porton Down, the results were quickly confirmed at other laboratories throughout the world. The samples were soon linked specifically to bees. Further research revealed that the yellow spots were actually bee excrement, released by the bees in mass cleansing flights.

Dr. Meselson of Harvard was among the early investigators of the bee pollen theory. Brookings analyst Elisa Harris describes the case presented by Meselson and others:

Meselson and the other scientists point first to various similarities between the yellow rain samples and bee feces: both have yellow spots of the same size, shape, appearance, and distribution; both have high concentrations of pollen; both contain bee hairs and fungal elements; and both test negative for the presence of protein, indicating that the pollen has passed through the digestive system of bees. They note, in addition, that many of the pollen types found in yellow rain samples come from plants common to Southeast Asia; that the pollen types found in these samples match those found in honey, honeybees, and honeybee feces collected in Thailand; and that no two yellow rain samples, or spots on the sample, contain the same combination of pollen, as is also the case with bee feces. In fact, every environmental sample of yellowish material from Southeast Asia examined for pollen has been found to contain it, including yellow rain samples obtained by the United States, the UN, Thailand, Canada, Australia, Sweden, and Britain. All of this suggests, Meselson and his colleagues claim, that the material known as yellow rain is actually Southeast Asian honeybee feces.[19]

"The discovery that the yellow rain in Southeast Asia was honeybee feces directly contradicted the administration's allegations of chemical warfare," wrote chemical and biological weapons expert Julian Perry Robinson and Jeanne Guillemin, along with Dr. Meselson, in 1987. "If the yellow rain was just bee feces, the administration's identification of the supposed toxic material was invalidated."[20]

Perry Robinson, Guillemin, and Meselson further reported that the "early reports of trichothecenes in the samples were totally unverified, and the corroboration that emerged later was tenuous and unreliable."[21] They cited various laboratory findings, including the results of an April 1987 study at Porton Down, that "despite what the U.S. government has previously asserted . . . indicate that trichothecenes do occasionally occur naturally in Southeast Asia."[22] Further, the authors point to "no clear evidence" to support allegations of chemical warfare through medical examinations of victims: "At no time, then or later, was any case documented in which diagnostic examination or autopsy provided clear evidence of exposure to chemical warfare agents."[23]

The validity of the testimony of alleged victims and eyewitnesses has also been questioned: "The supposed witnesses and the interpreters, often refugees themselves, generally knew in advance that the purpose of the interviews was to gather information about chemical warfare," Perry Robinson, Guillemin, and Meselson note. "The accounts were taken at face value; there was little attempt to double-check the stories by reinterviewing or to appreciate cultural differences between interviewers and respondents." The writers further indicated that "earlier interviews had failed to distinguish between first-hand observations and hearsay."[24]

Harris concurs in her own analysis of the administration's evidence:

In sum, one finds that the U.S. case for toxin warfare in Southeast Asia and Afghanistan is based on the following evidence: refugee and defector reports, many of which are inadequate both because of the source of the information and the manner in which it was obtained; a grand total of 26 positive samples from Southeast Asia, the results of which have never been confirmed by a second laboratory; one positive gas mask from Afghanistan that has been confirmed by other labs; and circumstantial evidence of Soviet involvement in the entire affair.

. . . if the United States had acquired a chemical munition or shell fragment from Southeast Asia and/or Afghanistan, its case would have been substantially strengthened. The fact that no such toxic-laden munition or shell fragment has ever been recovered from either region is highly significant, particularly in light of refugee reports of the dissemination of yellow rain from a variety of delivery systems, including rockets, bombs, mortar shells, land mines, and grenades. As the UN group investigating Iraqi chemical use in the [Iran-Iraq] Gulf war has shown, obtaining chemical munitions and fragments is not an impossible task, even in a conflict environment.[25]

"The charges of yellow rain warfare in Southeast Asia and Afghanistan have been at the center of the Reagan Administration's arms control noncompliance case against the Soviet Union," Harris further notes. "They have been used not only to justify increased chemical and biological warfare expenditures on the part of the United States, but also to weaken support for existing agreements in this area and perhaps future agreements as well.... Clearly ... the Reagan administration allowed its anti-Soviet zeal to take precedence over sound scientific principles."[26]

"A CHINK IN OUR ARMOR"

The Soviets vehemently denied the Reagan administration charges, countering that the accusations were "totally without substance" and a "malicious fabrication."[27] Nevertheless, the U.S. Department of Defense began to build its case to renew production of chemical weapons. In the report *A Chink in Our Armor: The Urgent Need for Chemical Weapons*, the Association of the United States Army was explicit in its opening commentary, warning: "The Soviets, or their surrogates, have gassed Afghans, Laotians, and Cambodians with impunity, and they will gas the U.S. and NATO forces, for we have allowed a natural distaste for this form of warfare to impede sound military planning and plain logic."

The association report, which called for modernizing the U.S. arsenal through production of binary nerve gas weapons, attributed the "marginal capability of the U.S. retaliatory stockpile" to the "cessation of munition production in 1969, and the conscious decision of three past administrations to refrain from making any improvements while pursuing total chemical weapon disarmament."[28]

President Reagan himself appealed to Congress in 1982 to approve production of nerve gas, and, although the request was denied, the administration pressed forward with its case in subsequent years. Secretary of Defense Caspar Weinberger cited a "current extreme unbalance" in early 1983, and called for congressional funding to begin production of binary nerve gas shells and bombs. "The Soviet Union possesses a formidable and expanding chemical warfare capability and continues to devote significant resources to research and development of chemical warfare programs," military officials told Congress. "To meet this threat, the Army must have a chemical retaliatory capability for deterrence and the capability to respond effectively with chemical weapons if deterrence fails."[29]

Susan Wright, a university instructor and editor of *Preventing a Biological Arms Race*, has noted that the Reagan administration's "presumption of Soviet military aggressiveness and the deterioration of East-West dialogue during his first years in office led to a policy characterized by rapid increases in spending on CBW programs, strong pressure on Congress to break the moratorium on chemical weapons production, and significant military assimilation of new biotechnology."[30]

In 1985, after repeated attempts by the administration to push through funding for new chemical weapons, Congress finally approved renewed production of binary nerve gas shells and bombs. Two years later, production

Gulf War troops drink from canteens attached
to their biological-chemical protection suits.
These suits were necessary because of threats
by Saddam Hussein to use chemical weapons.

World War I cavalrymen
and their horses wore
gas masks into battle.

The Stokes mortar shown here was used
primarily during World War I to deliver
chemical, smoke, and incendiary shells.

Soldiers with the U.S. Chemical Warfare Service
working in a lab at Edgewood Arsenal
around the time of World War I.

A view of Edgewood Arsenal about 1920,
showing the chemical munitions
plants, warehouses, and rail yards.

(Facing page) These giant storage tanks
at a 1937 I. G. Farben plant held ammonia
used in the manufacture of explosives.
One year earlier, Dr. Gerhard Schrader
discovered the deadly gas tabun
while he was working at a Farben plant.

(Above) In 1938, just prior to World War II,
the British donned gas masks and carried
on with regular activities such as shopping
while in the middle of drills for gas attacks.

American soldiers and their German prisoners wear gas masks while inspecting German gas bombs found in 1945. A trainload of some 55,000 bombs was captured.

(Above) Soldiers in the Vietnam War often patrolled streams and wooded areas that had been sprayed with Agent Orange. Many veterans who were exposed to the herbicide claim its long-term effects are disease and death. The subject is still highly controversial.

(Facing page) During World War II, the Japanese were well entrenched on Iwo Jima in blockhouses such as the one pictured here. U.S. military commanders thought the use of gas would be a way to force the Japanese out of their fortifications, but President Roosevelt would not agree to it.

(Above) Four thousand Kurds were killed
in 1988 when Iraq launched a gas attack against
the civilian population of Halabja, a Kurd village.

(Facing page) During the Vietnam War,
Agent Orange was widely sprayed from
aircraft to defoliate densely wooded areas.

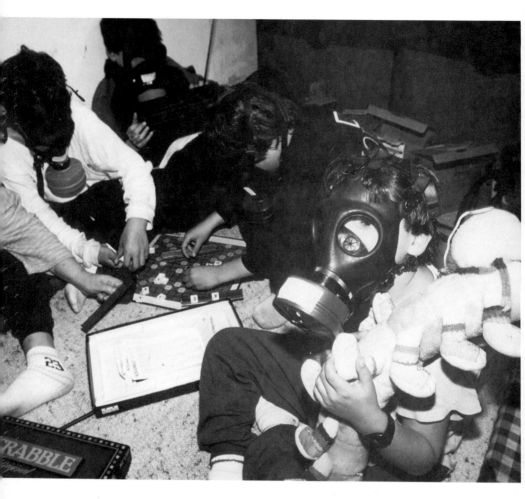

(Above) Israeli children wear gas masks as they play their usual games. As part of his Gulf War policy, Saddam Hussein threatened to attack Israel with chemical weapons.

(Facing page) The United States stockpiled chemical weapons during World War II to be used only in retaliation. These gas-filled shells at an eastern arsenal were checked regularly.

Soviet president Gorbachev and
United States president Bush signed
accords in June 1990 that set goals to
eliminate chemical weapons and
ban their future production.

began at the army's arsenal in Pine Bluff, where artillery shells were filled with an ingredient of GB (sarin), a nerve poison that becomes lethal when mixed with rubbing alcohol, then loaded into separate shells at another plant site. Ironically, production at Pine Bluff began a few months after President Mikhail Gorbachev announced that the Soviet Union had suspended its own production of chemical weapons.

1. "Chemical Warfare in Southeast Asia and Afghanistan," Report to the Congress from Secretary of State Alexander M. Haig, Jr., 22 March 1982, 6.

2. "Chemical Warfare in Southeast Asia and Afghanistan; An Update," Report from Secretary of State George P. Shultz, November 1982, 5.

3. Julian Perry Robinson, Jeanne Guillemin, and Matthew Meselson, "Yellow Rain: The Story Collapses," *Foreign Policy*, no. 68 (Fall 1987): 101.

4. Thomas Whiteside, "Annals of the Cold War: The Yellow-Rain Complex-I," *New Yorker*, 11 February 1991, 46.

5. Haig, "Chemical Warfare," 2.

6. Ibid.

7. Ibid., 6.

8. Ibid.

9. Ibid.

10. Ibid.

11. Ibid., 11.

12. Ibid., 6.

13. Ibid., 15.

14. Ibid.

15. Ibid., 6, 13.

16. Peter G. Keven and Makhdzir Mardan, "When Bees Get Too Hot, Yellow Rain Falls," *Natural History* (December 1990): 54.

17. Nicholas Wade, "Yellow Rain and the Cloud of Chemical War," *Science*, 27 November 1981, 1008–9.

18. Whiteside, "Annals of the Cold War," 58.

19. Elisa D. Harris, "Sverdlovsk and Yellow Rain: Two Cases of Soviet Noncompliance?" *International Security* 11, no. 4 (Spring 1987): 78–79.

20. Robinson et al., "Yellow Rain," 106–107.

21. Ibid., 107–108.

22. Ibid., 112.

23. Ibid., 114–115.

24. Ibid., 113.

25. Harris, "Sverdlovsk and Yellow Rain," 87–88.

26. Ibid., 94, 96.

27. Whiteside, "Annals of the Cold War," 60.

28. "A Chink in Our Armor: The Urgent Need for Chemical Weapons," Association of the United States Army, Arlington, Virginia, 5, 25.

29. "Administration Reopens Drive for Nerve Gas," *New York Times*, 20 February 1983.

30. Susan Wright, "The Buildup That Was," *Bulletin of the Atomic Scientists* (January/February 1989): 53.

AGENT ORANGE
AND VIETNAM

One of the great ironies of progress is that technological miracles designed to better life can, through ingenuity, be turned into highly effective weapons of destruction. So it was that in the search for a new and more powerful insecticide to protect food crops, a German chemist accidentally developed the world's first nerve gas.

Similarly, rapid U.S. advances in the development of agricultural herbicides, resulting in the production of super-strong agents that can discriminately kill plants or trees, led to a new form of warfare in Vietnam—one with lasting physical and psychological repercussions that remain unresolved to this day.

JUNGLE WARFARE

Vietnam was unlike any other war in which the United States had participated. The United States had the best fighting personnel, the best equipment, the best weapons, and the best training of any military organization in the world. On paper, it looked like a simple campaign:

drive the Vietcong out of South Vietnam and protect a democratic government.

In the field, however, it was another thing. This was not to be a war fought along classic lines, matching one army's strength against another's. This was to be more of a guerrilla action. America was fighting not only on the terrain of but also on the terms of the Vietcong. It was jungle warfare, where ambushes and hit-and-run tactics predominated.

Under such conditions, the great arsenal of the United States was to a large extent rendered ineffective. Further, the United States was at a disadvantage fighting in unfamiliar, hostile territory, a land the enemy knew intimately.

It took U.S. military leaders a long time to realize that classic maneuvers and strategies would not work in Vietnam. As a result, American casualties were abnormally heavy, and the war that most people initially thought would be won in months dragged on for years.

Eventually, strategists began to adapt somewhat to the situation. One of the first ideas on how to improve things was to seek ways to clear jungle areas from which the Vietcong staged bloody ambushes, such as heavily foliaged sections near supply lines and surrounding encampments and outposts.

In the early 1960s a team of chemical experts flew to Vietnam to test ways to destroy with chemicals the jungle trees and foliage so successfully used by the enemy for concealment. The experts not only concluded that the United States had the agents to do this job, but they also believed that no serious damage to Vietnamese agriculture or natural vegetation would result from the use of chemicals in this manner. Of course, their conclusions were based on the assumption that any defoliation campaign would be limited to relatively narrow strips of land near roads, highways, and power lines.

The idea of using chemicals for such purposes actually was not new with Vietnam. Toward the end of World War II, American scientists had investigated over 1,000 chemicals for their effects on vegetation and had developed at least three main agents. Had the war continued, U.S. authorities were considering using chemicals to destroy the rice crop, the staple of the Japanese diet, thus conceivably starving the country into surrender.

The question of whether or not use of chemical agents to defoliate a jungle violated the terms of the 1925 Geneva Protocol apparently was considered only briefly by the U.S. government before the agents were unleashed on Vietnam. No such weapons existed when the protocol was written; hence, there is no specific mention of herbicides or defoliants in the agreement. At the time this question came up, the U.S. State Department warned that other nations would look upon such use as violating the intention and spirit of the protocol, if not as a direct violation.

Such objections were brushed aside. The military apparently had been considering use of these agents for some time. One U.S. Army manual, *Military Biology and Biological Agents*, noted that chemicals have "high offensive potential for destroying or for seriously limiting the production of crops and for defoliating vegetation. . . . There are no proven defensive measures against these compounds. By the time the symptoms appear, nothing can be done to prevent damage. The compounds are detoxified in the soil after a period of several weeks to several months."

Another army training manual added: "Anti-plant agents are chemical agents which possess a high offensive potential for destroying or seriously limiting the production of food and [for] defoliating vegetation. These compounds include herbicides that kill or inhibit the growth of plants; plant growth regulators that either regulate or inhibit plant growth, sometimes causing plant death; dessicants that dry up plant foliage. . . . Military applications for anti-plant agents are based on denying the enemy food and concealment."

AGENTS WHITE, PURPLE, BLUE, AND ORANGE

As early as 1963, South Vietnamese aircraft began spraying U.S.-supplied chemicals on crops and jungle areas believed to be controlled by the Vietcong. By the mid-1960s, aircraft were dumping this poisonous rain over the whole of South Vietnam.

The actual compounds used were named Agents White, Purple, Blue, and Orange. White was used to control woody plants. Purple was a general defoliant. Blue was a contact herbicide containing cacodylic acid, used for grass control and the destruction of rice crops. The most notorious was Agent Orange. It was an herbicide containing a half-and-half mixture of normal butyl esters called 2,4-D and 2,4,5-T. Orange also contained a deadly toxin called dioxin. The substance is so lethal that only a few ounces in the water supply would be enough to destroy the entire population of New York City. Harvard University biochemistry professor Dr. Matthew Meselson calls it "the most toxic small molecule known to man."

Orange was designed for the control of trees, brush, and broadleaf weeds. One U.S. manufacturer of Orange warned on product labels: "Do not contaminate irrigation ditches or water used for domestic purposes. Caution: May cause skin irritation. Avoid contact with eyes, skin, and clothing. Keep out of reach of children. Application by airplane, ground rigs, or hand dispensers should be carried out only when there is no hazard from drift."

Agent Orange has a spectacularly devastating effect. It sends vegetation on what has been described as a "rapid and self-destructive growing binge." Plants doused with it literally explode, leaving a grotesque landscape where weeds grow into bushes and where trees, bowed down by the weight of their own fruit, lie rotting in the foul-smelling jungle. Vietnamese peasants called areas sprayed with Agent Orange "the land of the dead."

From a strategic point of view, the use of Agent Orange and other defoliant compounds was successful. Military commanders said areas sprayed with these chemicals reduced enemy ambushes by up to 90 percent. But the side effects of such usage may have been even more harmful. The problem was that at that time no one really knew what the long-term effects of such widespread sprayings would be.

The initial purpose as stated by the team of experts who looked into the matter in the early 1960s called for limited use of the agents, essentially on narrow strips of land. But as the war droned on, this aim seemed to have been forgotten. Agent Orange and other compounds began to be dumped indiscriminately over great areas of Vietnam. It saturated enemy and allied zones alike.

In the late 1960s, dozens of large C-123 transport planes, fitted with special spray tanks that held 1,000 gallons (3,785 liters) of these deadly chemicals, spewed their contents daily over the countryside. Ten thousand pounds (4,536 kg) of spray could cover up to 300 acres (121 ha) of jungle or rice paddies. Sometimes these planes hit their target areas; other times they did not. The lumbering C-123s made ideal targets for the Vietcong, and anxious pilots under heavy fire often unloaded the chemicals faster than plans called for. At times entire loads would be showered down in highly concentrated form on relatively small areas.

The concentrations of the chemicals themselves were at an estimated strength ten times more than what was called for in normal defoliage use. As a result, damage in many areas was far in excess of what had been expected. In some instances all woody plants were killed, including valuable commercial trees. The entire character of the countryside began to change. Despite military reports to the contrary, there was considerable evidence that rubber trees were destroyed, as well as fruit trees and vegetable farms.

By the late 1960s, over four million acres (1.6 million ha) had been defoliated, and nearly half a million acres (202,350 ha) of crops destroyed. Over 7,000 square miles (18,135 sq km)—about 10 percent of the whole of South Vietnam—had been sprayed, and there were reports that the neighboring lands of Laos and Cambodia also had received extensive coatings of the air-released chemicals.

SETTING A DANGEROUS PRECEDENT

Such massive use of toxic chemicals stirred a tidal wave of criticism, especially among the American and world scientific communities. Defoliants had never before been used on a scale as large as this. There was no way, scientists argued, to know whether or not the natural pattern of vegetation and wildlife—the very ecology of Vietnam—was being unalterably changed. Typical of this criticism were the comments in 1969 of Congressman Richard D. McCarthy of New York:

I find an anti-food campaign contrary to the principles of humanity. I consider the use of herbicides and defoliants—the new chemical weapons—on the scale that we have used them in Vietnam without knowing what the long-range consequences will be, to be irresponsible.

I also believe that it is one short step from the use of chemicals as an anti-vegetation or anti-crop weapon to the use of biological weapons for the same purpose. A rice blight or a plant blight, both biological agents, would be much more effective tools in defoliating a country and do not substantially differ in result from the use of chemicals. We run the risk of having such weapons used against our agriculture or that of our allies if we make anti-vegetation and anti-crop warfare an accepted practice.[1]

In September 1969, the American Society of Plant Physiologists sent the following letter to President Lyndon Johnson:

The undersigned Plant Physiologists wish to make known to you their serious misgivings concerning the alleged use of chemical herbicides for the destruction of food crops and for the defoliation operations in Vietnam.

We would assert in the first place that even the most specific herbicides known do not affect only a single type of plant. Thus a chemical designed to defoliate trees might also be expected to have some side effects on other plants, including food crops. Secondly, the persistence of some of these chemicals in soil is such that productive agriculture may be prevented for some years into the future, possibly even after peace has been restored. Thirdly, the toxicology of some herbicides is such that one cannot assert that there are no deleterious effects on human and domestic animal populations. The first and major victims of any food shortage or famine caused by whatever agent are inevitably children, especially those under five. This results mainly from their special nutritional needs and vulnerability to stress. Finally, it must be noted that the use of chemical herbicides, no matter how represented, is a resort to a kind of operation classed as biological warfare, and heightens the possibility of increasing the level of barbarity in an already terrible war.

That same month, a large group of distinguished American scientists, including several Nobel laureates, presented President Johnson with the following petition:

We, the American scientists whose names appear below, wish to warn against any weakening of the worldwide prohibitions and restraints on the use of chemical and biological weapons.

CB weapons have the potential of inflicting, especially on civilians, enormous devastation and death which may be unpredictable in scope and intensity; they have become far cheaper and easier to produce than nuclear weapons, thereby placing great mass destructive power within reach of nations not now possessing it; they lend themselves to use by leadership that may be desperate, irresponsible, or unscrupulous. The barriers to the use of these weapons must not be allowed to break down.

During the Second World War, the United States maintained a firm and clearly stated policy of not initiating the use of CB weapons. However, in the last few years the U.S. position has become less clear. Since the 1950s Defense Department expenditure on CB weapons has risen several fold—and there has been no categorical reaffirmation of the World War II policy.

Most recently, U.S. forces have begun the large-scale use of anti-crop and "non-lethal" anti-personnel chemical weapons in Vietnam. We believe this sets a dangerous precedent, with long-term hazards far outweighing any probable short-term military advantage. The employment of any one CB weapon weakens the barriers to the use of others. No lasting distinction seems feasible between incapacitating and lethal weapons or between chemical and biological warfare. The great variety of possible agents forms a continuous spectrum from the temporarily incapacitating to the highly lethal. If the restraints on the use of one kind of CB weapons are broken down, the use of others will be encouraged.

Therefore, Mr. President, we urge that you:

Institute a White House study of overall Government policy regarding CB weapons and the possibility of arms control measures with a view to maintaining and reinforcing the worldwide restraints against CB warfare.

Order an end to the employment of anti-personnel and anti-crop chemical weapons in Vietnam.

Re-establish and categorically declare the intention of the United States to refrain from initiating the use of chemical and biological weapons.

There is no real way, even today, years after the sprayings took place, to know the long-range effects. Will millions of acres of once-arable Vietnamese farmland remain a desolate wasteland? Will future generations eating crops raised on such acreage be doomed to disease and death? It may take decades to know for sure.

Defoliant agents were not the only chemicals the United States used in its desperate attempts to win the Vietnam War. A new order of tear gases was introduced as early as 1965. Robert McNamara, then secretary of defense, called these "riot-control gases," and an attempt was made to disassociate them from "regular chemical weapons."

These gases, code-named CN, CS, and DM (which was the most toxic) were more powerful than any previous tear gases. They entered the lungs and could cause second-degree burns. The tear gases were used principally to rout the enemy from caves and bunkers, and were dropped in bombing raids preceding infantry assaults.

Military commanders argued that this was a "humanitarian" use of chemicals to reduce casualties. Otherwise, it was said, the Vietcong would be blown up in the caves. Millions of pounds of these gases were produced for use in Vietnam, and their effectiveness was reported to be successful. The *Army Times* noted: "Entrenched areas that have successfully resisted both aerial and artillery fire have been reduced in an hour or two by combining the use of CS with maneuver and firepower."

Still, there was widespread criticism of the use of these gases. Some argued that even though tear gases are not known as lethal, their application technically violated the no-first-use (of chemical weapons) policy long espoused by the United States. Others feared their introduction would encourage enemy uses of chemical weapons. Said Congressman McCarthy of New York: "I believe this [use of tear gas in Vietnam] to be a clear violation of the gas ban in the Geneva Protocol of 1925."[2]

A DEADLY LEGACY

Today, the United States continues to wrestle with the legacy of Agent Orange use in Vietnam. Most important, there is the burning and still undecided question of whether Agent Orange and its deadly ingredient, dioxin, have long-term effects on humans. Dioxin is a highly toxic cancer-causing substance. It is known to cause severe skin disorders and is suspected of causing various diseases. There are reports that the instances of stillbirths in Vietnam doubled in areas sprayed with Agent Orange.

One major epidemiological study conducted by Vietnamese scientists, as reported by *Science* magazine, turned up evidence of an increase in the incidence of congenital abnormalities among children whose fathers were exposed to herbicides during the Vietnam War. Following reports of a dramatic increase in birth defects in rural Vietnam, fears grew about the risks of dioxin. The military halted the use of the defoliant in 1970.

Many Vietnam veterans are convinced that the ailments they now suffer from can be directly traced to instances of exposure to Agent Orange during the aerial sprayings. The incidence of cancer among these men appears to be higher than the national average. Robert Harris and Jeremy Paxman, in *A Higher Form of Killing*, reported that of children fathered by men exposed to Agent Orange, "no less than 40,000 are said to suffer from serious birth defects."[3]

Additionally, there appears to be a larger than normal incidence of kidney, bladder, colonic, and testicular cancers among Vietnam veterans who were exposed to Agent Orange. Thousands have reported suffering severe chloracne rashes, piercing migraine headaches, and recurring bouts of nausea, vomiting, dizziness, and diarrhea. They also suffer from violent rages, mood swings, memory lapses, numbness, shortness of breath, intolerance to alcohol, sudden debilitating weight losses, photosensitivity, and premature aging.

Consequently, in 1981 more than 20,000 U.S. servicemen, 4,000 Australians, and nearly 2,000 New Zealanders who were subjected to Agent Orange sprayings in Vietnam brought a class-action suit against the seven major U.S. companies that produced the chemical for the Department of Defense. The suit contended that these companies knew years before the chemical's use in Vietnam that there were hidden dangers to dioxin exposure. Experiments have determined that dioxin in amounts as small as five parts per trillion can cause cancer in rats. Researchers at the University of Nebraska found that men who served in areas sprayed with Agent Orange have retained significant levels of dioxin in their fatty tissue.

The Vietnam veterans pointed to a case in 1982 in which a jury in Edwardsville, Illinois, awarded forty-seven railway workers $58 million after they were exposed to a solvent that contained dioxin during the cleanup of a tank car rupture near Sturgeon, Missouri. Many of the workers complained of the same symptoms as those described by the vets: frequent nausea, loss of sex drive, and excessive tiredness. These workers were exposed to dioxin of only twenty-two parts per billion. This, say lawyers for the Vietnam veterans, was 1,000 times less than the exposure of the soldiers in Southeast Asia.

Still, the evidence remains inconclusive. A spokesperson for the Dow Chemical Company, one of the Agent Orange manufacturers, said the company maintains "overwhelming scientific data" proving that exposure to small amounts of dioxin is harmless and that veterans were not exposed to levels high enough to have caused permanent damage.[4] Dow also maintains that any higher rate of illness among vets could be the result of a combination of drugs administered in Vietnam and bacteria found in the soil there. Finally, Dow argues, even if Agent Orange is found to have caused serious illness, responsibility lies with the government, not the manufacturer, which simply followed government guidelines in preparing the defoliant.

Dow and six other manufacturers of dioxin agreed to a settlement, however, with the Vietnam veterans. According to a May 7, 1984, out-of-court agreement, the companies consented to pay $180 million over the next twenty-five years. The amount, which was the largest damage claim ever in a product liability case, was approved in federal court the following September. Several consumer and veterans groups expressed disapproval at both the settlement amount and the fact that a verdict was not drawn from the case. Under the terms of the settlement, spouses and children of veterans, and the manufacturers themselves, were permitted to sue the government. The Justice Department, however, responded in a September 7, 1984, court brief that it would fight any Agent Orange suits brought against it. Government representatives argued that the seven chemical companies should bear liability exclusively, claiming that they were by no means under "compulsion to manufacture the herbicide."

The $180 million settlement is being distributed in cash payments to those 20,000 to 50,000 veterans who are totally disabled and to the survivors of those who died. About $50 million has been set aside for special programs, including counseling, job training, rehabilitation, and legal assistance, for veterans suffering from the effects of Agent Orange.

Still, the size of the settlement—which averaged less than $10,000 per claim—left many of the veterans bitter. The fact that liability was not proven further exacerbated the victims' anger and frustration. Scientific studies have for the most part failed to confirm a direct link between Agent Orange and the many serious ailments reported by veterans.

Among the most controversial investigations was a $63 million study—eventually canceled after several years of research—performed by the Centers for Disease Control (CDC) in Atlanta. According to the CDC's study director, Dr. Vernon Houk, Pentagon information provided to the CDC was too sketchy to assemble the required documentation on troop locations and potential exposure to Agent Orange. "If we could find a population of people who were exposed in sufficient numbers, we would have proceeded with our study," Houk says. "We just simply could not find them."[5]

Retired admiral Elmo R. Zumwalt, who, as the former chief of Naval Operations ordered much of the Agent Orange spraying in Vietnam and who is now serving as a special assistant to the Veterans Administration, charged that the CDC's work in the Agent Orange study was "a fraud." Several critics questioned whether the CDC might have been bowing to pressure from the Reagan administration, which may have wanted to avoid huge liability claims. In his fifty-five-page report on the study, Zumwalt charged:

> ... it should come as no surprise that those familiar with the CDC's work found little credence in the conclusions reached by the CDC in its recently released Selected Cancers study. Even though CDC has previously stated that it believes exposure to Agent Orange is impossible to assess, it found no difficulty in reporting to the press upon the release of the Selected Cancers Study that exposure to Agent Orange does not cause cancer. This conclusion was reached despite the fact that the CDC made no effort to determine, through military records or blood/adipose-tissue tests, if study subjects were, indeed, exposed to dioxin; nor did the CDC attempt to verify exposure to Agent Orange of these study subjects who actually contracted cancerous diseases.
>
> Unfortunately, political interferences in government-sponsored studies associated with Agent Orange have been the norm, not the exception.[6]

Zumwalt's role in pursuing aid for veterans exposed to Agent Orange represents one of the more bitter ironies of the Vietnam saga. As the navy's top commander in Vietnam, he ordered massive quantities of Agent Orange sprayed over the Mekong Delta region. His son, Elmo Zumwalt III, was a navy lieutenant serving in the area. In 1988, the younger Zumwalt died of a rare lymphoma. His father believes that Agent Orange is directly responsible for his son's death.

Veteran's interest groups continue to press for compensation and acknowledgment from the government that the prevalence of ailments should be officially linked to exposure to Agent Orange. Among the more recent studies, an air force investigation released in March 1991 revealed links between Agent Orange and some ailments, including diabetes, but not cancer or other serious diseases often cited by the veterans. And as recently as July 1991, the Department of Veterans Affairs said Vietnam veterans exposed to Agent Orange could receive disability benefits for a nerve disease. However, the VA denied links between Agent Orange and lung cancer, and has not yet decided if there is a link between the herbicide and diabetes.

Significant progress, however, has included the Agent Orange Act of 1991, which was signed by President George Bush in February of that year after receiving unanimous congressional approval. The bill provides permanent disability benefits to those veterans who are suffering from two rare forms of cancer—non-Hodgkin's lymphoma and soft-tissue sarcoma—and cloracne, a skin disease. The bill also calls for the National Academy of Sciences to perform independent scientific reviews to determine whether other medical conditions may have been caused by Agent Orange and other herbicides used in Vietnam. "This legislation relies on science to settle the troubling questions concerning the effect on veterans of exposure to herbicides—such as Agent Orange—used during the Vietnam era," President Bush said upon signing the bill.

"The issue of the effects of exposure to Agent Orange is one of deeply held, but divisive, beliefs," he continued. "My administration has stated many times one overriding goal in this area—providing the truth to Vietnam veterans about the effects of exposure to Agent Orange."

1. Richard D. McCarthy, *The Ultimate Folly: War by Pestilence, Asphyxiation and Defoliation* (New York: Alfred A. Knopf, 1969), 50.

2. Ibid., 50.

3. Robert Harris and Jeremy Paxman, *A Higher Form of Killing* (New York: Hill and Wang, 1982).

4. Pete Earley, "Viet Vets' Herbicide Suit Settled," *Washington Post*, 8 May 1984.

5. George J. Church, "A Cover-up on Agent Orange?" *Time*, 23 July 1990, 28.

6. "A Disturbing Bias," *American Legion Magazine* (August 1990): 56.

"A ROUGH AND READY EQUALIZER"

A non-Arab Muslim people, with a population of approximately 15 million, the Kurds inhabit the mountains and plateaus of a region known as Kurdistan, or "Land of the Kurds," stretching through Iran, Iraq, Syria, Turkey, and the Soviet Union. Once a nomadic group tending flocks of sheep and goats, the Kurds have now settled into village life and modern employment, forced over time to abandon their traditional way of life by the influences of the nations they occupy.

Troubled by the division of their native land into regions within several modern states, the Kurds have long sought autonomy. At times, they have paid for their uprisings through the indiscriminate slaughter of their population at the hands of retaliatory rival forces, most notably, Iraq.

HALABJA: "A GRAVE VIOLATION"

No episode speaks more clearly of Kurdish suffering than the March 1988 bombing of Halabja, a thriving trade center in northern Iraq near the Iranian border. In a brutal assault toward the close of the Iran-Iraq War, Iraq dropped canisters of mustard gas, cyanide, and nerve gas on the unsuspecting and unprepared town, which had recently been overtaken by the Iranian Revolutionary Guard. As many as 5,000 Kurds were killed, including women and children—some literally stopped in their tracks as they walked along the village streets.

"They were slow and painful deaths," reported Isabel O'Keeffe in the *New Statesman Society*. Describing the devastating attack, which also injured another 7,000 civilians, she added:

> By attacking the bone marrow, thus destroying the body's ability to make white cells and to fight off infection, mustard gas eventually kills those who do not suffocate in the bombardment. The more visible effects are huge, ulcerated blisters that form mostly in the armpit and groin. Victims of the even more lethal nerve gas first experience blurred vision. Then, as if a clamp were being tightened around their chests, they fight for breath. Death is usually caused by asphyxiation after severe attacks of muscle spasm, vomiting, and diarrhea. A UN team sent to examine the victims found conclusive evidence that mustard gas had been used, and indications of nerve gas, too.[1]

Five months later, Iraqi warplanes dropped mustard gas on the village of Mesi, also in northern Iraq. According to a survivor, most of the 900 inhabitants of Mesi and nearby villages were killed. Others escaped—bearing the gruesome wounds inflicted by the poison gas—to a refugee camp across the Turkish border.

Following the Mesi attack, Secretary of State George Shultz called the Iraqi attacks against the Kurds abhorrent and unjustifiable, and immediately called for the imposition of economic sanctions against Iraq. The Reagan administration also labeled the Halabja massacre "a particularly grave violation" of the Geneva Protocol, but little occurred in the way of reprisal against Iraq by the international community following either episode.

In fact, the poison gas episodes met with little outcry from around the world. The horrible slaughter of unarmed Kurdish civilians, which had followed brutal Iraqi mustard gas attacks against Iranian soldiers as early as 1983, went largely unanswered, in part because many nations did not want to appear to be siding with Iran in the conflict. Most notably, Iraq escaped without heavy criticism during the Paris Conference on the Prohibition of Chemical Weapons in January 1989, where a final statement issued by participants referenced only "recent violations such as have been confirmed by competent bodies of the United Nations."

That a nation could inflict such devastation through the merciless use of poison gas—generated with documented Western assistance, no less—without international condemnation was a clear indication that the threat of chemical warfare had indeed become a reality. It was also a signal to other Third World nations that chemical warfare could be employed without fear of international reprisal. As Secretary Shultz put it in September 1989, "For a long while, this genie had been kept in the bottle . . . [now] it's out."[2]

THE POOR MAN'S ATOMIC BOMB

While international focus had for several years centered on suspected Soviet use of poison gas in Southeast Asia and Afghanistan, many nations were quietly building up chemical and biological warfare capabilities. The Central Intelligence Agency estimates that as many as twenty nations have developed or are pursuing development of chemical weapons.[3] Simple and inexpensive to manufacture, with readily accessible technology and ingredients,

CBW offers a "rough and ready equalizer to the nuclear weapons of technologically advanced countries," reported *The New York Times*, adding, "once one country gets them, fearful neighbors may follow."[4]

"Proliferation of weapons of mass destruction in the Third World will be one of our major challenges in the future," stated CIA director William Webster in September 1990:

> It has already happened. We gathered up so many weapons and weapons became so readily available that artillery and rockets and so on became stockpiled all over the world. And those gradually found their way into Third World countries. But as this was happening, we were also seeing that weapons such as chemical weapons and biological weapons became the subject of both acquisition and indigenous research and development and production. . . . So suddenly this sleepy, Third World area becomes significant to the United States and its allies.[5]

Destruction of Iraqi chemical arms factories and stockpiles was thus a primary objective of the U.S. and coalition forces during the Persian Gulf War. By the end of January 1991, during the first week of air attacks, at least a dozen weapons facilities had been destroyed and much of the nation's ability to produce chemical and biological weapons had been eliminated.

The New York Times reported, however, that military intelligence analysts feared that the elimination of "thousands of tons of chemical and biological weapons already stockpiled at hundreds of sites across Iraq" would be a "much more difficult task" for the allied forces.[6] Even if all such storage sites had been discovered and destroyed, destruction of chemical and biological weapons stockpiles might have contaminated crops and water supplies, and potentially proven deadly to nearby populations.

Indeed, postwar investigations by United Nations inspectors tasked with overseeing arms elimination in Iraq revealed that the nation's chemical weapons stockpile was several times larger than Iraqi officials had admitted. By July 1991, UN inspectors had found 46,000 chemical shells and warheads—more than four times what Iraq originally reported; and 3,000 tons of raw materials for chemical weapons, instead of 650 tons. The inspectors also confirmed that, as much of the world had feared, the chemical warheads were loaded with the lethal nerve gas sarin, and that some Scud missiles contained these warheads.[7]

EXPORTING THE DEADLY EXPERTISE

Ironically, an influx of ingredients and technology from Western nations has aided many Third World countries, including Iraq, in their quest for chemical arms. Among the many reports:

- "Chemical and biological weapons development in Iraq has been done largely with European scientists and technicians, many from West Germany," reported *Aviation Week and Space Technology* in August 1990, adding that "most of the casings, shells, and bombs in which the chemical weapons are packaged for delivery have been purchased by Iraq from Spain."[8]
- Iraq received thiodiglycol, a key ingredient for manufacturing mustard gas, from Phillips Petroleum in Oklahoma. According to Paris-based *L'Express*, "five hundred tons were delivered through a Dutch firm, KBS Holland BV, to a 'pesticide' plant in the Iraqi town of Samarra. Only after a second order was delivered in 1984 did Phillips begin to have doubts." *L'Express* went

on to report that "West Germany is the all-time champion in the chemical business," and that "other chemical traders spotted by the CIA include the Belgians, the Brazilians, the Dutch, the French, the Indians, and the Swiss."[9]

- Another American corporation, Alcolac International of Baltimore, Maryland, was convicted in 1989 of violating U.S. export laws by shipping thiodiglycol to Iran. One account stated that "court records show that Alcolac, aware of U.S. restrictions on the sale of the chemical to Iran, sold the chemical to a West German company, knowing that it would be re-exported to Iran."[10]

- "Foreign assistance was of critical importance in allowing Syria to develop its chemical warfare capability," testified CIA director Webster before the Senate Foreign Relations Committee in March 1989. "West European firms were instrumental in supplying the required precursor chemicals and equipment. Without the provision of these key elements, Damascus would not have been able to produce chemical weapons."[11]

- Webster also testified that "firms and individuals from Western Europe were key to the supply of chemical process equipment, chemical precursers, and technical expertise" for the development of Iraq's largest chemical weapons manufacturing complex, near Samarra. Webster noted that Iraq's program had by then become so well established, it was "far less dependent on foreign assistance."[12]

The construction and operation of a large so-called pharmaceutical plant in Rabta, near the Libyan capital of Tripoli, also drew international attention in the late 1980s as a suspected chemical weapons plant—believed to be the largest of its kind in the world. Built with extensive West German assistance, most notably from the chemical manufacturing giant Imhausen, the plant was completed in 1989 and was believed to have initiated production of poison gas weapons in early 1991.[13] In March 1991, the United States announced its suspicions that Libya was even digging a bunker around the perimeter of the plant site to protect chemical arms manufacturing operations from air attack.

Debate over the nature of the plant at Rabta underscores the difficulty frequently faced in locating and verifying chemical and biological arms production. "It would have been virtually impossible for Libya to harness the technologies necessary to build and operate such facilities without the assistance of foreign companies and personnel from several West European and Asian countries," Webster reported in his testimony to the Senate Foreign Relations Committee.

"Assistance provided by foreign suppliers, many of whom were fully aware of the intentions of the Middle East countries to produce chemical weapons, has been the key element that has enabled these nations to develop a capability to produce chemical weapons within only a few years . . . without this assistance, these Middle East countries would have been unable to produce chemical weapons." He went on to note that exported assistance has included "technical and operations expertise, constructing production facilities, supplying precursor chemicals, supplying production equipment, supplying parts for munitions, and training personnel."[14]

Concern over Western assistance to Iraq and other Third World countries in their quests for chemical and biological arsenals has prompted several nations and arms control proponents to call for an international ban on the exportation of precursor ingredients and technology and to initiate export curbs independently. Under the Toxic Substance Control Act of 1976 and the Arms Export Control Act of 1976, for example, the United States restricted the sale of numerous chemicals to several "suspect" nations, including Iraq, Iran, Libya, and Syria. These controls were tightened considerably in early

1991, when President Bush approved legislation that expanded the number of chemicals on the export ban list, and strengthened sanctions against foreign nations and individuals suspected of CBW activity.

Still, such controls may be difficult to monitor. Many of the precursor ingredients are legitimately used in other applications. The chemical ingredients required to produce mustard gas, for example, are similar to those required for manufacturing drugs, pesticides, and plastics.

Several groups are working to eliminate the transfer of key chemicals and equipment, however, and are sharing information and pursuing stringent controls. The Australia Group, for example, is an association of nineteen Western nations and a delegate from the European Community that was formed in 1985 with the objective of developing strategies and policies to limit the flow of precursor ingredients and other assistance to nations seeking to build CBW arsenals. The group meets twice a year in Paris to discuss export restrictions and share information on ingredients and technology.

The Chemical Manufacturers Association (CMA), which represents approximately 95 percent of the chemical production capacity of the United States, has also pledged its support in the prevention of proliferation through export regulations. CMA has provided information on ingredients and technology, helped develop methodology for monitoring shipments and production, and arranged for a trial inspection of a chemical plant to validate procedures for verification purposes.

THE TERRORIST THREAT

The most stringent of export controls—even the realization of an international agreement to halt production and use of chemical and biological weapons—may not be sufficient to restrain the use of poison gas or toxins by another threatening force: terrorists. Increasingly, experts fear that CBW may become the "weapon of choice" for international terrorist forces. "A suitcase 'forgotten' on a subway, a train, or an airport is enough to do the job," cites *L'Express*.[15] The realization, for example, that a few cells of a biological contaminant might infect an urban water supply system and kill hundreds of thousands within hours is a horrifying one to governments and a powerful negotiating point for terrorists.

Many of the common advantages of CBW development and use are critical to terrorist elements: the ability to work quickly and secretly, in cramped facilities, with limited funds and technical expertise.

"I would be more concerned about this [CBW] risk than that the terrorists would acquire a nuclear capability," CIA director Webster stated in March 1989. "Even if you could steal a nuclear weapon, it is much too difficult to acquire that and use it, when there are so many other weapons of terrorism readily available. The advantage to a terrorist of chemical weaponing, particularly biological weapons, is that the instrument of destruction can be very small and easily concealed, and utilized in places like the ventilation system of a key building. . . . The potential for lethal consequences is very high, without all of the difficulties that would be encountered in trying to do the same kind of thing with a nuclear threat."[16]

"Why would terrorists want to go beyond more conventional weapons and enter the realm of mass destruction weapons?" Joseph D. Douglass, Jr., and Neil C. Livingstone theorized in *America the Vulnerable: The Threat of Chemical and Biological Warfare*. "Because the essence of terrorism is to intimidate and to sow fear, the most horrific and intimidating weapons are those capable of mass destruction: nuclear, chemical, and biological. . . . Governments are as terrified of weapons of mass destruction as is the man on the street. . . . C/B weapons are the stuff of nightmares."[17]

Despite progress toward a global ban on chemical weapons, many nations still fear that CBW is an everyday concern, and one that, whether state-sponsored or the work of terrorists, may spell disaster with little or no warning. Some countries—Israel, for example—have equipped citizens with protective gear and provided assistance with creating sealed environments in case of emergency. Israeli citizens frequently underwent alarming emergency drills during the Persian Gulf War in early 1991 in the midst of Iraqi air attacks. Though Iraq limited its air raids to conventional warheads, the threat of chemical attacks was a frightening prospect.

"The threat of chemical or biological warfare has not disappeared," said Graham A. Castillo, executive secretary of the Puerto Rico Chemists Association in May 1991. The association's announcement that it was joining forces with the Puerto Rico Medical Association to study the effects of CBW shows the rising concern many groups are experiencing in assessing national vulnerability to CBW.

"We are not ready to handle the potential dangers of an attack," said Dr. José C. Roman, president of the medical association. "We have the responsibility to alert the medical profession and the general public. . . . Puerto Rico is a major strategic military point for the U.S. As such the island should never consider itself completely immune from attack." The associations called for medical readiness, emergency shelters, and contingency plans in the event of an attack.[18]

The recent horrors witnessed as a result of CBW attacks in the Middle East, and the potential for large-scale chemical and biological weapons attacks during the Persian Gulf War, are indeed alarming reminders of this viable threat. Will a global ban—if achieved—ease the fear of national leaders and the international public?

1. Isabel O'Keeffe, "Flanders Field Revisited," *New Statesman Society*, in *World Press Review* (March 1989): 12.

2. Russell Watson with John Barry, "Letting a Genie Out of a Bottle," *Newsweek*, 19 September 1988, 30.

3. Senate Committee on Foreign Relations, "Chemical and Biological Weapons Threat: The Urgent Need for Remedies," S. Hrg. 101–252, January 24, March 1, and May 9, 1989, 29.

4. "At the Summit: Verify, but Trust," *New York Times*, 2 June 1990.

5. "What Makes Hussein So Dangerous?" *U.S. News & World Report*, 10 September 1990, 40.

6. Eric Schmitt, "A Search and Destroy Priority: Unconventional Iraqi Munitions," *New York Times*, 30 January 1991.

7. Frank J. Prial, "Iraq Disclosed Only One-Quarter of Its Chemical Arms, U.N. Finds," *New York Times*, 31 July 1991, A1.

8. "Iraqi Chemical Weapons Development Program Relied on Western European Assistance," *Aviation Week & Space Technology*, 30 August 1990, 26.

9. Elie Marcuse, "An Equality of Terror," *L'Express*, in *World Press Review* (March 1989): 18.

10. Patrick G. Marshall, "Obstacles to Bio-Chemical Disarmament," *Editorial Research Reports*, 29 June 1990, 372.

11. Senate Committee on Foreign Relations, "Chemical and Biological Weapons Threat," 32.

12. Ibid., 31.

13. Michael Wines, "U.S. Hints at Chemical Arms Bunker in Libya," *New York Times*, 7 March 1991.

14. Senate Committee on Foreign Relations, "Chemical and Biological Weapons Threat," 31.

15. Marcuse, "An Equality of Terror," 18.

16. Senate Committee on Foreign Relations, "Chemical and Biological Weapons Threat," 41–42.

17. Joseph D. Douglass, Jr., and Neil C. Livingstone, *America the Vulnerable: The Threat of Chemical and Biological Warfare* (Lexington, Mass.: D. C. Heath, 1987), 15.

18. P. J. Ortiz, "Chemical and Biological Warfare Dangers Discussed," *San Juan Star*, 9 May 1991.

TREATIES MADE, TREATIES BROKEN

When French and German armies signed the Strassburg Treaty in 1675, they agreed that "no side should use poisoned bullets." This treaty was the first such formal agreement specifying and prohibiting a form of chemical warfare in modern history. Since that time governments have similarly attempted to restrict or ban chemical and biological weapons through international treaties.

In the latter half of the nineteenth century, these efforts became more concentrated, beginning with the prohibitions detailed at the 1874 Brussels Convention. It was decided here that nations should not use poison or poisoned weapons during war, and that arms, projectiles, or other weapons should not cause unnecessary suffering.

In 1899, at the first international peace conference in The Hague, a similar prohibition was proposed. Signatory nations were to "abstain from the use of projectiles, the object of which is the diffusion of asphyxiating or deleterious gases." The Hague Gas Declaration, signed by the United States, France, Britain, Germany, Russia, Italy, and other nations, was confirmed at the 1907 Hague Conference.

The foresight of these attempts at deterring the development and employment of chemical weapons (biological weapons had yet to be specifically addressed) was not enough to prevent their use during World War I. The devastation and suffering incurred, however, spurred postwar restraint attempts, and disarmament quickly became a major international concern. The Versailles Treaty of 1919, which formally ended the war, prohibited the manufacture of chemical weapons in Germany, Austria, Hungary, and Bulgaria. It also banned the export of such weapons to these countries, and prohibited the use of gas for other countries as well.

Postwar developments increased the potential danger of chemical warfare. In 1922, during the Naval Conference in Washington, D.C., the United States, Britain, France, Italy, and Japan agreed that "the use in war of asphyxiating, poisonous or other gases and all analogous liquids, materials or devices" should be prohibited by international law. France, however, would not ratify the agreement due to its opposition to an unrelated segment of the treaty, and the treaty did not take effect. The Washington Treaty was successful, though, in setting precedent for later negotiations, especially during the 1925 Geneva Conference.

THE GENEVA PROTOCOL

The newly assembled League of Nations met in Geneva, Switzerland, to consider a report that had appeared the previous year about the effects of chemical and biological weapons. Compiled at the request of the League, the report made it clear that chemical weapons were both powerful and dangerous. During the ensuing discussions, the United States sought to establish a prohibition of the exportation of gases. A majority agreed, however, that such a ruling would be unfair to those countries not producing chemical weapons. France then proposed a prohibition of the use of poisonous gas, and Poland followed with a suggestion to prohibit bacteriological weapons as well. Both of these points were adopted in the protocol.

The nations present (the Soviet Union did not attend) drafted a proposal, largely based on the provisions of the Washington Treaty, which again banned the use of chemical weapons. The document read, in part:

> Whereas the use in war of asphyxiating, poisonous or other gases, and of all analogous liquids, materials or devices, has been justly condemned by the general opinion of the civilized world; and
>
> Whereas the prohibition of such use has been declared in Treaties to which the majority of Powers of the world are Parties; and
>
> To the end that this prohibition shall be universally accepted as a part of International Law, binding alike the conscience and practice of nations;
> Declare;
>
> That the High Contracting Parties, so far as they are not already Parties to Treaties prohibiting such use, accept this prohibition, agree to extend this prohibition to the use of bacteriological methods of warfare and agree to be bound as between themselves according to the terms of this declaration. . . .

The Geneva Protocol then went to the various nations for ratification. By World War II, forty-three countries had signed. The United States and Japan were two significant exceptions. Heavy lobbying by the American Chemical Society and the military's Chemical Warfare Service caused Congress to refrain from pushing the protocol through—a delay that would last fifty years. Other nations, including Great Britain, France, and the U.S.S.R., signed after the addition of two clauses that permitted them the use of chemical weapons if the enemy used them first, while also nullifying the protocol restrictions if the enemy were not a party to the treaty. The protocol became, effectively, a no-first-use treaty. Significantly, the agreement did not prohibit the production and stockpiling of chemical and biological weapons.

Although the protocol was largely adhered to, even through World War II, a few highly publicized incidents of noncompliance did occur—specifically, the use of poisonous chemicals during the Italian invasion of Ethiopia and incidents of chemical warfare in China at the hands of the Japanese.

There were no significant incidents of biological or chemical warfare recorded during World War II, but many would argue that this was largely due to both factions' strong fear of reprisal. Although the Axis powers actually possessed a substantial lead in chemical warfare development, they believed the Allies capable of equally devastating retaliatory measures. Germany chose not to introduce its weapon.

POSTWAR PRODUCTION

Production was renewed on a large scale in the United States in the 1940s. During World War II the United States opened thirteen new chemical warfare plants. President Franklin Roosevelt was dead set against the use of these weapons but, fearing Japanese gas attacks in the South Pacific, felt compelled to order their production.

In 1946 the Chemical Warfare Service, which had reached a wartime unit strength of 69,000 troops, was renamed the Chemical Corps. Research and development continued, although little was said about it. Still, the official U.S. position remained in concert with the 1925 Geneva Protocol: the United States would not be the first to use such weapons in time of war; it would use them only in retaliation.

Use of atomic weapons at the close of the war did much to overshadow the biological and chemical warfare issue. Indeed, until 1952, during the Korean War, the Geneva Protocol was not in the forefront of international affairs. Then the Soviet Union accused the United States of employing both chemical and biological weapons in Korea and China. Although they were unable to provide sufficient evidence in the matter, the Soviets proposed a resolution to require all United Nations members to ratify the 1925 protocol. The resolution did not pass, but the discussions did serve as a reminder both of the severity of chemical weapons and of the need to further formalize and expand restrictions on their use.

Slowly, quietly, the United States policy on no-first-use of chemical weapons, in accordance with the nation's protocol position, began to erode. Congressman Richard McCarthy of New York said, "The growth of our gas and germ arsenal was as much a product of neglect at the top policy levels of government as it was of secrecy."[1] He pinpointed the year 1956, during President Dwight Eisenhower's administration, as a major turning point in American policy on CBW.

McCarthy claimed that it was during this year that proponents of poison gas in the United States began gradually to change CBW policy from one of no-first-use to one that "refused to preclude the possibility of the initiation of gas or germ warfare."

Indeed, alterations of U.S. Army manuals of that era reflect this trend. One such manual was changed to read, cryptically, "The decision for U.S. forces to use chemical and biological weapons rests with the President of the United States." More blatantly, the army's *Field Manual on the Law of Land Warfare* was rewritten to include a statement that read: "The United States is not a party to any treaty, now in force, that prohibits or restricts the use in warfare of toxic or nontoxic gases . . . or of bacteriological warfare. . . . The Geneva Protocol for the prohibition in war of asphyxiating, poisonous or other gases, and of bacteriological means of warfare . . . is . . . not binding on this country."

This marked a dramatic turnaround in U.S. policy on CBW, but it had been done so secretly that hardly anyone, including critics of chemical and biological warfare, even knew about it at the time.

By the 1960s, the Department of Defense had a number of major CBW sites scattered throughout the United States and overseas. These included:

- Edgewood Arsenal, a research and development center just 20 miles (32 km) northeast of Baltimore, Maryland
- Fort Detrick, a research and development center for biological weapons located near Frederick, Maryland
- Rocky Mountain Arsenal, a major chemical weapons production site only a few miles northeast of Denver, Colorado
- Newport, in western Indiana, a nerve gas production site
- Pine Bluff Arsenal, near Little Rock, Arkansas, a major CBW production and storage site
- Dugway Proving Grounds, Utah, the military's largest gas and germ testing station
- Desert Test Center, Fort Douglas, Utah, another large testing station
- Fort McClellan, Alabama, site of specialized CBW training for U.S. servicemen and -women
- Oakland, California, site of a large naval biological laboratory
- China Lake, California, testing site for naval CBW weapons

■ Eglin Air Force Base, Florida, testing site for airborne CBW weapons systems

Additional tests have been conducted at sites at Fort Hua-Huachuca, Arizona; Fort Greeley, Alaska; Fort Clayton, Panama; and on Eniwetok atoll in the Pacific. Also, at Plus Island, near New London, Connecticut, extensive biological testing has been carried out. CBW storage sites include Blue Grass Army Ammunition Depot, Lexington, Kentucky; Tooele Army Ammunition Depot, Tooele, Utah; and Umatilla Army Ammunition Depot, Umatilla, Oregon.

Further, by the 1960s dozens of the nation's leading colleges and universities had contracted with the U.S. government to conduct research on CBW. Several of the country's largest companies also carried out such research.

By the mid-1960s word of all this effort, despite its secretive nature, began slipping out. In 1966, during the Vietnam War, Hungary and several other Communist countries began to criticize the United States over its use of riot-control gases and herbicides in Vietnam. The United States insisted that the Geneva Protocol did not apply in such instances of limited application, and a three-year debate flourished within the United Nations.

Early in 1968, an incident occurred that had perhaps as much influence on swaying public opinion against the continuing CBW buildup as anything else. At 5:30 P.M. on Wednesday, March 13, an Air Force jet roared over a large circular target area laid out on the Utah desert floor. During a test mission near Dugway Proving Grounds, 320 gallons (1,211 liters) of the deadly nerve gas VX were sprayed from the aircraft. At the end of the test run, however, two high-pressure dispensers failed to snap firmly shut. As a result, the deadly VX continued to pour out, outside the target area, and wind gusts carried it as far as 45 miles (72 km) away.

Within days, thousands of sheep in the Skull and Rush valleys died. Incredibly, the military first said that no outdoor gas tests had been carried out recently. But as the evidence of what happened began to mount, the army slowly changed its position (although it did not fully admit the extent of the accident until a year later) and eventually paid the farmers more than half a million dollars in damages.

This shocking incident and a number of other accidents and near misses created a groundswell of public opinion against chemical and biological development in the United States. Still, even as late as 1969, a statement issued through the office of Secretary of Defense Melvin Laird declared: "It is the policy of the U.S. to develop and maintain a defensive chemical-biological capability so that our military forces could operate for some period of time in a toxic environment if necessary; to develop and maintain a limited offensive capability in order to deter all use of chemical and biological weapons by the threat of retaliation of kind."

But Laird and the military were overruled in 1969 by President Richard Nixon, who, sensing the public mood, announced a no-first-use chemical warfare policy. Nixon also disavowed any American intent ever again to make biological weapons. All such existing weapons were ordered destroyed, and the president said U.S. forces would never use them, even in retaliation against an enemy that used them against the United States. Nixon's stand was reinforced in April 1972 when eighty-seven nations signed a treaty banning biological weapons, including their development and retention.

While Nixon's edict and the Biological Weapons Convention Treaty effectively put a halt to biological weapons work, the U.S. military continued to find loopholes involving certain chemical weapons—especially the tear gases and defoliation agents used in Southeast Asia. Clauses permitting such usage and reserving a right to retaliate in kind if any enemy used gas warfare were added to the Geneva Protocol, which Nixon resubmitted to the Senate in November 1969. It was the first submission of the protocol in twenty-three years.

The Senate pushed for further clarity of terms and lingered over the protocol until December 1974, when members voted to accept it. By April 1975, fifty years after the original agreement, the United States had finally ratified the Geneva Protocol.

REBUILDING THE ARSENAL

"President Reagan formally told Congress yesterday that production of new lethal nerve gas weapons 'is essential to the national interest,' clearing the way for an end to a nearly thirteen-year-old U.S. moratorium on their manufacture," reported a February 1982 *Washington Post* article, which continued: "Reagan contended that U.S. production on a new generation of weapons is needed to deter possible Soviet use of chemicals in a war."

Following the collapse of CBW arms reduction negotiations in the early 1970s, and reports that the Soviet Union was using chemical weapons in Southeast Asia and Afghanistan during the mid- and late 1970s, the U.S. position on CBW began to swing once more from disfavor to a more active status. While the Reagan administration favored a universal ban on chemical weapons, 1984 budget requests included over a billion dollars for chemical weapons programs—protective measures, maintenance, and the development of new nerve gas shells and artillery shells. The administration's support of a strong course of deterrence through chemical weapons buildup sparked intense congressional and public debate.

"If the chemical threat from the Soviet Union is as dangerous and real as argued," wrote Congressmen Dante B. Fascell and John E. Porter in a *Washington Post* editorial, "then the priorities of our chemical program should be the protection of our troops, the maintenance of our current adequate retaliatory stockpile and the pursuit of a verifiable arms control ban on chemical weapons."[2]

"The issue is not whether to develop a 'new type' of chemical weapon or a more lethal one," countered Senators John Glenn, Barry Goldwater, Sam Nunn, and John Warner in another *Post* column. "The issue that Congress will soon be deciding is whether to keep our chemical deterrent in the old and increasingly dangerous unitary canisters or whether to put it in the new and safer binary shells."[3] After three years of denying funding for new chemical arms production, Congress approved the program in 1985.

THE CHEMICAL WEAPONS CONVENTION

The Reagan administration is to be credited, however, with actively supporting a global ban on chemical weapons. The United States has been a leading participant in ongoing chemical arms negotiations in Geneva, which have been underway for over two decades as part of the United Nations Conference on Disarmament. In 1984, then vice-president George Bush presented a draft disarmament treaty to the delegates that provided "an important turning point," notes John Isaacs of Council for a Livable World. "That draft became the basis for negotiating a 'rolling text,' a draft treaty that has been undergoing continuous modification." Isaacs further describes the nature of the agreement:

> The essential aim of the treaty is an agreement by all countries to refrain from developing, producing, acquiring, stockpiling, and retaining chemical weapons, or transferring them, directly or indirectly, to any country. Within 30 days of taking effect, the convention would require each country

to reveal how many chemical weapons it has, and where. Signatories would have to begin destroying existing stockpiles within a year and complete the job within 10 years. All chemical weapons plants would cease production immediately and be completely dismantled within 10 years.

To ensure compliance, the draft convention provides for a three-tier verification system. First, international teams would inspect all chemical weapons stocks and factories, both immediately and during the destruction process. Second, measures would be taken to verify that the civilian chemical industry is not producing chemical weapons. For example, observers would conduct systematic on-site inspections and would carefully monitor the production of industrial chemicals that could be used in weapons. Third, "challenge inspections" would be used to deter violations and investigate suspected infractions. If international observers suspected illegal activity, they could demand to visit a plant on short notice.[4]

The challenge inspections are among the heavily debated points of contention in the draft treaty. In 1990, the United States, which originally proposed the inspections in its 1984 proposal, began to hedge on this aspect. "What relative weight do you give to two competing national interests?" asks Ambassador Steven J. Ledogar, the U.S. delegate to the Geneva talks. ". . . With anytime-anywhere inspections, you could suddenly find out that a national security facility, which is extremely sensitive, could be compromised by just very basic knowledge of its existence."[5]

Ledogar adds, however, that the nations are moving closer to resolution of this point, through possible adoption of a "managed access" approach that would permit protection of national security secrets while allowing challenge inspections to take place. A U.S. proposal, submitted in July 1991 and supported by Britain, Australia, and Japan, called for a new challenge inspection plan and attempted to move the negotiations forward, but many analysts believed the proposal fell short in outlining a program to detect violators.

"The proposal would let a challenged country stall for days without allowing inspectors to glimpse a chemical-weapons site," writes Amy E. Smithson, a senior associate at the Henry L. Stimson Center in Washington, D.C., and a verification specialist. She adds that, "inspectors might never be able to step inside the gates of facilities where cheating is suspected," and that a challenged party might opt instead to allow only aerial observation or observation from an "elevated platform."[6]

Another difficult issue centered on a U.S.–Soviet proposition that would enable countries to retain 500 tons of chemical agents until all nations capable of producing chemical weapons had signed the agreement— much like the terms of the bilateral agreement between the superpowers. Disarmament proponents argued that this measure ran counter to the spirit of the talks, as did another U.S. position supporting preservation of the right to retaliate in kind to a chemical attack. In May 1991, President Bush reversed the U.S. position on both of these proposals, a dramatic move hailed by many experts as a major step toward resolution of the global ban.

Representatives at the Geneva talks and chemical weapons experts around the world are now strongly encouraged by the Chemical Weapons Convention proceedings. "After more than a generation of international negotiations to ban the possession and production of chemical weapons, a breakthrough might be brewing," reported the Arms Control Association in May 1991.[7]

Many issues have yet to be resolved. "Postponing hard decisions and advancing positions that hinder the negotiations could mean that the opportunity to achieve an important goal will be lost forever," cautions Isaacs. "Given the political will, an international convention could be completed in the next year or two. But if a treaty is indefinitely postponed, and if other developing countries are tempted to follow Iraq's and Libya's lead, the world may not be able to return the chemical weapons genie to the bottle."[8]

"A TRAILBLAZING AGREEMENT"

While the Geneva talks continue, the United States and former Soviet republics work toward the initial steps outlined in the June 1990 bilateral accord. The process has not been without obstacles, however, and will likely be "overtaken" by the multilateral ban.

"It takes an awful lot of money to destroy chemical weapons," Ambassador Ledogar notes. "It takes an awful lot of confidence on the part of people who live near the destruction facilities that the destruction experts know what they are doing. The environmental problems that the Soviet Union has had, and the political protests, have made implementation of Soviet CW destruction plans quite difficult."[9]

Still, the bilateral agreement is, according to the U.S. administration, a "trailblazing agreement," calling for sweeping reductions in current stockpiles, to be conducted in a "safe and environmentally sound manner." Major terms of the agreement include the following:

- Destruction of at least 50 percent of declared stocks by the end of 1999
- Declared stocks to be reduced to 5,000 agent tons by 1992
- Both countries will stop producing chemical weapons upon entry into force of this agreement, without waiting for the global chemical weapons ban

- On-site inspections during and after the destruction has taken place
- Annual exchanges of data on the stockpile levels to facilitate monitoring of the declared stockpiles
- Both countries will cooperate in developing and using safe and environmentally sound methods of destruction
- The United States and the Soviet Union will take steps to encourage all chemical weapons–capable states to become parties to the multilateral convention. Both countries took an initial step in this direction by exchanging data on declared chemical weapons stockpiles in December 1989, and by initiating verification experiments to build confidence and gain experience for a chemical weapons ban treaty.

The accord further states that:

> The bilateral United States–Soviet agreement was designed to provide new impetus to the conclusion of a comprehensive, verifiable global chemical weapons ban at the earliest possible date. Toward that end:

- Both countries have agreed to accelerate their destruction of chemical weapons under a global chemical weapons convention so that by the eighth year after it enters into force, the United States and the Soviet Union will have reduced their declared stocks to no more than 500 agent tons.
- The United States and the Soviet Union will propose that a special conference be convened at the end of the eighth year of a multilateral convention to determine whether participation in the convention is sufficient to complete the elimination of chemical weapons stocks over the following two years.

"The most striking fact about this agreement was that it was reached, despite the fact that its terms will be difficult to verify," commented a *New York Times* editorial about the bilateral accord. "It shows that the two old adversaries have now developed a measure of trust."[10]

"AN UNUSUAL AND EXTRAORDINARY THREAT"

"I, George Bush, President of the United States of America, find that proliferation of chemical and biological weapons constitutes an unusual and extraordinary threat to the national security and foreign policy of the United States and hereby declare a national emergency to deal with that threat."

With that statement, issued on November 16, 1990, President Bush ordered a number of measures designed to aid in stemming the proliferation of chemical and biological weapons until such time that a multilateral accord eliminated them from the earth.

In addition to a statement that pursuit of a global treaty would be a "top priority of the foreign policy of the United States," these measures included the prohibition of "the export of any goods, technology or services" that would "assist a foreign country in acquiring the capability to develop, produce, stockpile, deliver, or use chemical or biological weapons." Further, the emergency action outlined sanctions to be taken against foreign countries or persons with respect to CBW proliferation, including the following:

- No foreign assistance other than assistance intended to benefit the people of that country directly
- No loan or financial or technical assistance by international financial institutions, nor any credit or financial assistance by any U.S. department or agency
- Prohibition on arms sales
- Import and export restrictions
- Termination of air landing rights

On March 7, 1991, President Bush announced expanded U.S. export controls that applied to "equipment, chemicals, and whole plants that can be used to manufacture chemical or biological weapons, as well as to activities of U.S. exporters or citizens when they know or are informed that their efforts will assist in a foreign missile or chemical or biological weapons program."

The new regulations increased the list of potential chemical or biological arms ingredients subject to control from eleven to fifty and created stringent new licensing rules. The regulations also included tighter controls for those countries suspected of having unconventional weapons programs, largely in the Middle East and Southwest Asia.

"Saddam Hussein's use of chemical weapons against his own citizens, his use of Scud missiles to terrorize civilian populations, and the chilling specter of germ warfare and nuclear weapons have brought home the dangers proliferation poses to American interests and global peace and stability," President Bush said. "Our continuing efforts to stem the spread of weapons of mass destruction will contribute to the construction of a new world order."[11]

1. Richard B. McCarthy, *The Ultimate Folly: War by Pestilence, Asphyxiation and Defoliation* (New York: Alfred A. Knopf, 1969), 24.

2. Dante B. Fascell and John E. Porter, "New Nerve-Gas Weapons That We Don't Need," *Washington Post*, 17 June 1985.

3. John Glenn et al., "Chemical Weapons: The Real Issues," *Washington Post*, 21 May 1985.

4. John Isaacs, "Banning Chemical Weapons," *Technology Review* (October 1990): 36.

5. "Ambassador Stephen J. Ledogar: Closing in on a Chemical Weapons Ban," interview with Jack Mendelsohn and Lee Feinstein, *Arms Control Today* (May 1991): 3.

6. Amy E. Smithson, "Chemical Inspections: On the Outside Looking In?" *Bulletin of Atomic Scientists* (October 1991): 23–24.

7. "Ambassador Stephen J. Ledogar," Weapons Ban," 3.

8. Isaacs, "Banning Chemical Weapons," 40.

9. "Ambassador Stephen J. Ledogar," 7.

10. "At the Summit: Verify, But Trust," *New York Times*, 2 June 1991.

11. "White House Statement of Weapons of Mass Destruction," 7 March 1991.

DISPOSAL:
THE ENVIRONMENTAL
CHALLENGE

Eight hundred miles southwest of Honolulu lies Johnston Island, a remote, 2-mile-long (3.2 km) sliver of land that is part of Johnston Atoll, a cluster of tiny islands encircled by a coral reef in the South Pacific. An unincorporated U.S. territory, Johnston Atoll was designated a National Wildlife Refuge in 1926 and is home to humpback whales, sea turtles, and hundreds of species of birds and fish.

In addition to the marine wildlife, Johnston Island is populated by some 1,300 U.S. soldiers and civilians charged with operating the Johnston Atoll Chemical Agent Disposal System (JACADS), a prototype chemical weapons destruction plant. The $240 million plant is the site of the U.S. Army's sixteen-month "operational verification test program," launched in June 1990, for the incineration and disposal of chemical munitions and agents.

Johnston Island has been the storage site of mustard and nerve gas weapons since 1971, when a U.S. stockpile of approximately 13,000 tons—some 300,000 pieces of rockets, artillery shells, mines, and bombs—was removed from Okinawa. In late 1990, the U.S. stockpile of chemical weapons stored in Germany—approximately 100,000 pieces—was also transferred to the island.

The JACADS test program is to be followed by destruction of the complete arsenal stored on Johnston Island. The army will not initiate testing for additional disposal programs (to be conducted at eight continental U.S. sites) until initial operations at Johnston Island have been completed and analyzed. With pressure mounting as a result of the congressional mandate and the U.S.– Soviet agreement, both requiring that the bulk of the nation's chemical weapons stockpile be destroyed before the end of the decade, the army is carefully scrutinizing the JACADS program.

ARMS CONTROL VERSUS THE ENVIRONMENT

The Pacific community, including New Zealand, Micronesia, and Hawaii, is also closely watching operations at Johnston Island. Pacific nation leaders have vigorously registered their concern over the selection of the tiny island for further storage and disposal of hazardous materials. Further, environmentalists throughout the world have registered alarm over the potential dangers surrounding the transport, storage, and destruction of chemical weapons on Johnston Island.

The environmental action group Greenpeace has been a leading critic of the U.S. Army's plans for incineration, arguing among other concerns that the process will release dioxin and furan (a flammable liquid) into the air—some of the "most dangerous chemicals known to man," according to attorney Paul Spaulding III.[1] Spaulding represents the Sierra Club Legal Defense Fund, which, on behalf of Greenpeace, filed suit against the Department of Defense in 1990 to halt the incineration program.

Such challenges to the implementation of chemical and biological weapons destruction, including citizen, environmental, and political opposition, are today a serious threat to the successful completion of chemical arms elimination required by the U.S.–Soviet pact, and ultimately, to the prospect of a global agreement. "In the past, arms control people and environmentalists have been on the same side," says Elisa Harris of the Brookings Institution. "With incineration, these groups are on opposing sides. Arms control people are saying, 'Let's go forward.' Environmentalists are saying, 'Let's put it off until the technology is right.' These groups may be raising enough challenges to make it impossible to meet domestic or international mandates."[2]

THE CHEMICAL STOCKPILE DISPOSAL PROGRAM

Prior to 1969, the U.S. Army disposed of obsolete chemical arms through deep ocean dumping and open-pit burning. The National Academy of Sciences (NAS) eventually concluded that ocean dumping was hazardous, however, and a congressional ban was imposed on this form of disposal in 1972. By 1984, NAS had formally recommended high-temperature incineration as the optimum method for disposing of chemical weapons.

The incineration process employed on Johnston Island involves breaking down the munitions into their component parts. "Once disassembled," a May 1990 congressional report states, "the agent and the chemical munition components are burned separately in four specially designed furnaces. The liquid furnace destroys the lethal agent. The deactivation furnace burns explosive and propellant materials. The metal parts furnace decontaminates projectile and bulk munition bodies by evaporating and burning the residual agent. The trash and dunnage created by the operations are destroyed in the dunnage incinerator."[3]

"In 1983 we went to the National Academy of Sciences, the most prestigious independent body in the U.S.," says Brig. General Walter Busbee, program manager of the chemical militarization program, "and presented the technologies that had been evaluated over a 20-year period from the late '60s through the early '80s. And they said, 'Direct incineration is the best prospect for the safest and most environmentally sound method of disposing of these agents.' "[4]

Environmental groups disagree. "We think incineration is the wrong technology," says Sebia Hawkins, co-director of the Pacific campaign of Greenpeace. "We can't just shove this stuff into incinerators. Toxics escape no matter what precautions you take, and the emissions settle on the ocean. We believe they can find a more suitable method."[5]

That belief led to the Greenpeace lawsuit to halt JACADS operations until a full environmental impact statement could be completed and alternative destruction methods studied. (Greenpeace has dismissed the army's 1990 environmental impact statement as inadequate.) In addition to the organization's concern over the potential release of toxic compounds, such as dioxin and furan, during incineration, the group charges that a "sea surface microlayer could help to concentrate and recirculate toxic, persistent, bioaccumulative substances . . . which may then find their way into the marine food chain."[6]

"The U.S. Army has failed to conduct a comparable analysis of alternate technologies for detoxification of chemical weapons, based on available scientific literature," noted a Greenpeace review of the JACADS environmental impact study. The review recommended that "existing chemical weapons stockpiles remain segregated in above-ground, monitored, retrievable storage," and that "strict precautionary measures" be taken to avoid environmental damage from accidents or natural disasters.[7]

EXAMINING THE ALTERNATIVES

Greenpeace further noted that "new scientific information indicates that alternate detoxification technologies exist which the U.S. Army has failed to investigate, and in comparison with incineration, they are relatively benign environmentally. The technology for neutralization of the chemical weapons is well known and, in fact, has been developed by the Army."[8]

Chemical neutralization, cited by Greenpeace as a "well-proven" technology, is among the leading alternatives to incineration. While the U.S. Army has opted for the development of incineration plants in light of NAS recommendations, neutralization continues to be researched and may eventually emerge as the preferable method. According to NAS experts, the process is currently too slow and complicated, with "excessive quantities of waste that cannot be certified to be free of agent," and requiring "higher capital and operating costs."[9] Greenpeace counters that the "excessive waste" is actually "relatively benign" neutralized salts, and that "neutralization technology coupled with new research on alternative technologies for the degradation of the neutralized salts or liquids must be considered by the Department of Army."[10]

Brig. General Busbee concedes that the Greenpeace argument has "some interesting engineering and scientific concepts," and that other concepts and technologies may "prove out in 10 or 20 years. But we do not have, in my judgment and in the directive the Congress has given the Army, 10 or 20 years to dispose of these weapons. Some of them are leaking. The greatest hazard to the environment at Johnston Island is the continued storage of the munitions there."[11] Harvard biochemistry professor Matthew Meselson also points out that the high-temperature incineration of chemical weapons will cause

116

less pollution than many urban refuse incinerators because the chemical reactions are more predictable and more easily monitored.[12]

Transport of chemical weapons to the Johnston facility also presented a critical concern, as environmentalists feared a potential shipping mishap or accident, or possibly a terrorist attack. In 1990, under pressure from the West German government, the United States initiated withdrawal of a chemical weapons stockpile there, ahead of a previously agreed-upon 1992 deadline. Transport involved placing the nerve gas shells in vapor-proof steel containers, which were then encased in U.S. Army ammunition shipping containers, or MILVANS. The shells were then transported by truck, rail, and ship to Johnston Atoll.

Although the government reported that the transfer to Johnston Atoll "was conducted successfully, safely, and in accordance with [the Department of Defense's] overall schedule,"[13] the army has determined that the destruction of remaining U.S. stockpiles should take place at the eight continental munitions sites where the remaining chemical weapons are currently stored: Tooele, Utah; Anniston, Alabama; Pine Bluff, Arkansas; Umatilla, Oregon; Pueblo, Colorado; Newport, Indiana; Lexington-Blue Grass, Kentucky; and Aberdeen, Maryland.

According to the military's analysis, on-site destruction "(1) is the best choice from a public health perspective; (2) reflects a realistic appraisal of our ability to mitigate accidents; (3) is less vulnerable to terrorism and sabotage; and (4) is far less complex in terms of logistics, including security and emergency response."[14] Still, the government admits, "construction could be delayed at three sites [Lexington-Blue Grass, Aberdeen, and Newport] because of community opposition to the on-site incineration of lethal chemicals and at two sites because of added restrictions imposed by regulatory agencies."[15]

SAFETY: THE BOTTOM LINE

Addressing the October 1990 Pacific Island Nations–United States summit, President Bush attempted to reassure representatives that the U.S. planned to dispose of "only the chemical munitions from the Pacific theater currently stored at Johnston Atoll, any obsolete materials found in the Pacific Islands, and those relatively small quantities shipped from Germany." He added that "these munitions will be destroyed safely on a prioritized schedule . . . once the destruction is completed, we have no other plans to use Johnston Atoll for any other chemical munitions purpose or as a hazardous waste disposal site. . . . The safeguards we're employing ensure that there will be no associated environmental damage."

Still, many residents of the Pacific states remain concerned. An accidental nerve gas leak at a JACADS incinerator in December 1990 did little to quell their fears. The U.S. Army claimed that the amount of gas that escaped into the atmosphere was only one-twelfth of the level allowed by the federal government, and "not a reportable chemical event." According to Lt. Colonel Leland Nakai, U.S. Army Pacific chemical staff officer, "The plant operation has been accident free. We've had no exposures to people. And of course the bottom line out there is plant safety."[16]

Soviet attempts to implement a chemical weapons destruction program have met with equally vigorous opposition from citizens and environmentalists. A chemical destruction plant near the city of Chapayevsk, designed to destroy up to 5 tons per day of the Soviet stockpile, never opened as a result of citizen protests. The Soviets have been forced to consider other options in order to initiate elimination of their arsenal by the end of 1992 under the terms of the U.S.–Soviet accord.

"Greenpeace and other environmentalists must carefully weigh the benefits to world peace and the environment that would flow from the total destruction of chemical weapons and a perpetual ban on their acquisition and use, against the temporary and perhaps marginal environmental gains to be made from disrupting that process," writes Trevor Findlay, senior research fellow at the Peace Research Center of the Australian National University. "From an arms control perspective, major disruption or a complete halt to the planned chemical process could have major consequences. . . . If the U.S.–Soviet accord is not implemented successfully, progress toward a global ban will almost certainly be slowed."[17]

Yet, as Greenpeace and other environmental groups assert, safer, more reliable destruction methods must continue to be researched. If feasible, these methods should ultimately supersede current incineration plans at the continental U.S. sites. "While too late for the plant at Johnston Atoll," Findlay writes, "the eight continental U.S. destruction sites could still use [the new destruction techniques]. Clearly, greater international cooperation is needed to achieve the safest possible chemical weapons destruction method worldwide, and the recent U.S.–Soviet accord is a first step in that direction, calling for technological cooperation in the two sides' destruction efforts."[18]

1. Janice Otaguro, "The Worst That Could Happen," *Honolulu* (March 1991): 56.
2. Susan E. Davis, "The Battle Over Johnston Atoll," *Washington Post*, 9 April 1991.
3. "Chemical Weapons: Obstacles to the Army's Plan to Destroy Obsolete U.S. Stockpile," General Accounting Office, May 1990, 12.
4. Otaguro, "The Worst That Could Happen," 56.
5. Eddie Sanders, "Plant Incinerates Chemical Weapons," *Pasadena Star News*, 16 February 1991.
6. Trevor Findlay, "Chemical Disarmament and the Environment," *Arms Control Today* (September 1990): 15.

7. "Greenpeace Review of Johnston Atoll Chemical Agent Disposal System (JACADS) Final Second Supplemental Environmental Impact Statement (June 1990) for the Storage and Ultimate Disposal of the European Chemical Munition Stockpile," 9 July 1990, 6, 16, 19.

8. Ibid.

9. Findlay, "Chemical Disarmament," 12.

10. "Greenpeace Review," 20.

11. Otaguro, "The Worst That Could Happen," 56.

12. Findlay, "Chemical Disarmament," 15.

13. "Chemical Warfare: DOD's Successful Effort to Remove U.S. Chemical Weapons From Germany," General Accounting Office, February 1991, 2.

14. Findlay, "Chemical Disarmament," 12.

15. "Chemical Weapons," 25.

16. Otaguro, "The Worst That Could Happen," 56.

17. Findlay, "Chemical Disarmament," 16.

18. Ibid.

TOWARD A
GLOBAL BAN

"Today I want to announce steps that the United States is ready to take, steps to rid the world of these truly terrible weapons, toward a treaty that will ban, eliminate, all chemical weapons ten years from the day it is signed." On September 25, 1989, President Bush pledged his total support for a chemical weapons ban—and a willingness to allow the United States to lead by example in this critical effort—in an address to the United Nations General Assembly.

Since that address, events in the chemical arms negotiations theater have occurred in swift and dramatic fashion. The U.S.–Soviet bilateral accord, signed by the two presidents in June 1990, set unprecedented goals for eliminating chemical weapons arsenals and banning production. And the thirty-nine-nation chemical arms negotiation proceedings in Geneva have taken a promising turn toward the long-hoped-for global ban, despite continuing discussion on the final few points of contention.

Today, as the Geneva talks move forward, the United States and the former Soviet republics are at work on the fundamentals of CBW disarmament, including construction of disposal facilities; development of environmental safeguards; and finalization of thorough, mutually agreed-upon inspection procedures. The superpowers have also been joined by several other nations in attempting to prevent proliferation of chemical and biological weapons through expanded export controls and the development of sanctions against countries who engage in CBW development. While incidents of chemical warfare have gone largely unanswered in the recent past, it is unlikely, given the current focus on CBW elimination efforts, that such episodes would occur without sweeping international admonition and public outcry today.

Still, many analysts fear that unless the global ban is reached soon, the opportunity may be lost. "If we don't move very quickly [toward a global agreement]," says Congressman Martin Lancaster of North Carolina, "about all we'll be able to do is make sure our troops are well trained and well equipped . . . and just let everybody have their chemical weapons and hope that when the war breaks out we're capable of protecting our troops."[1]

"The most crucial political question remains whether all states will adhere to the convention," says John Isaacs of Council for a Livable World. "Although the Chemical Weapons Convention would treat all nations equally, no one can be sure that countries such as Iraq, Iran, Libya, Israel, and South Africa will sign the treaty. These countries have so far given mixed signals."[2]

Some critics charge that even if the global ban were to be finalized in the near future, it would be untenable—quite simply because it would be impossible to verify compliance. Other analysts are more optimistic. "An international convention will not provide an absolute guarantee against the spread of chemical weapons," concedes Isaacs, "but it will greatly diminish the likelihood of their proliferation and use." He adds:

Countries will have less incentive to develop these weapons if they know that most other nations, large and small, are eliminating their stockpiles and agreeing not to produce any new ones. A convention will also lessen the perception of chemical arms as a legitimate form of warfare. And it can enhance international efforts to establish export controls to prevent developing countries from acquiring chemical and technical assistance for producing such weapons. If the convention provides tough sanctions against violators, it could discourage future Iraqs and Libyas.[3]

Isaacs points out that even if the Geneva participants arrive at a treaty, U.S. Senate ratification would still be a "major hurdle." The Chemical Weapons Convention could be subjected to "intense scrutiny," he says, a debate that would likely focus on the issue of verification. "Ultimately the president will have to make a strong case on behalf of the treaty," Isaacs notes, adding:

The president helped his cause at the United Nations in September 1989, when he declared that verification of a chemical weapons ban was possible: "We know that monitoring a total ban on chemical weapons will be a challenge. But the knowledge we've gained from our recent arms control experience and our accelerating research in this area makes me believe that we can achieve the level of verification that gives us confidence to go forward with the ban."

The chemical industry's support of the projected treaty will also be an important boost during Senate consideration. It was largely because of industry opposition that the Senate delayed ratification of the 1925 Geneva Protocol until 1975. In October 1987, the board of directors of the

American Chemical Manufacturers Association endorsed the ban on chemical weapons. Since then, CMA representatives have offered technical advice and support to the U.S. negotiating team.

One more factor in the convention's favor: the Senate has never been enthusiastic about funding new U.S. production of chemical weapons. During the Reagan administration, there were three separate tie votes on whether to approve production. Even then, the White House had to lobby hard for weapons production as a bargaining chip for securing a chemical treaty in Geneva.[4]

Given the commitment now put forth by President Bush—demonstrated by the U.S.–Soviet accord, his declaration in November 1990 of a "national emergency" regarding the threat of CBW proliferation, and his May 1991 agreement to key concessions that eliminated the "security stockpile" and the right to retaliate in kind—the United States does appear to be willing to support this critical arms elimination effort.

Most experts agree that a combination of strategies— the global ban, export controls, a strong challenge inspection and verification program, sanctions against offenders, and a moral obligation on the part of all nations to speak out and take action against CBW violators—is the best prospect we have for eliminating chemical and biological weapons altogether and securing the "new world order" President Bush envisions.

1. Lee Feinstein, "Speak Loudly, Carry a Small Stick," *Bulletin of the Atomic Scientists* (December 1990): 49.
2. John Isaacs, "Banning Chemical Weapons," *Technology Review* (October 1990): 38.
3. Ibid., 35.
4. John Isaacs, "Can a Chemical Weapons Treaty Survive in the Senate?" *Technology Review* (October 1990): 39.

FOR FURTHER READING

Brown, Frederic J. *Chemical Warfare: A Study in Restraints*. Princeton, N.J.: Princeton University Press, 1968.

Clarke, Robin. *The Silent Weapons*. New York: David McKay, 1968.

Cole, Leonard A. *Clouds of Secrecy: The Army's Germ Warfare Tests Over Populated Areas*. Totawa, N.J.: Rowman & Littlefield, 1988.

Douglass, Joseph D., Jr., and Neil C. Livingstone. *America the Vulnerable: The Threat of Chemical/Biological Warfare*. Lexington, Mass.: Lexington Books–D.C. Heath and Co., 1987.

Harris, Robert, and Jeremy Paxman. *A Higher Form of Killing: The Secret Story of Chemical and Biological Warfare*. New York: Hill and Wang, 1982.

Hersh, Seymour M. *Chemical and Biological Warfare: America's Hidden Arsenal*. Indianapolis: New York, Bobbs-Merrill, 1968.

McCarthy, Congressman Richard D. *The Ultimate Folly*. New York: Knopf, 1969.

Rose, Steven, ed. *Chemical and Biological Warfare*. Boston, Mass.: Beacon Press, 1968.

DISCARD

INDEX

Regular loan : 2 weeks
A daily fine is charged for each overdue book.
Books may be renewed once, unless reserved
for another patron.
A borrower is responsible for books damaged
or lost while charged on his card